Miss Daisy's
HEALTHY SOUTHERN COOKING

To: Ann
Happy Cooking!
Daisy King
6/13/2013

Miss Daisy's HEALTHY SOUTHERN COOKING

❧ DAISY KING ❧

CUMBERLAND HOUSE
NASHVILLE, TENNESSEE

Published by
Cumberland House Publishing
431 Harding Industrial Drive
Nashville, Tennessee 37211

Cover design: Gore Studio, Inc.
Text design: Mary Sanford

Library of Congress Cataloging-in-Publication Data
King, Daisy, 1945-
  [Miss Daisy cooks light]
  Miss Daisy's healthy southern cooking / Daisy King.
      p. cm.
  Previously entitled: Miss Daisy cooks light.
  Includes bibliographical references and index.
  ISBN 1-58182-395-9 (pbk. : alk. paper)
  1. Low-fat diet—Recipes. 2. Low-fat diet—Recipes. 3. Salt-free diet—Recipes.
4. Cookery, American—Southern style. I. Title.
  RM237.7.K56 2004
  641.5'638—dc22
                                                              2004002330

Printed in the United States of America
1 2 3 4 5 6 7—10 09 08 07 06 05 04

This book is dedicated to my sons,
William Kevin King and Patrick Leslie King,
who continue to give me their love and support
in my daily walk through life.

Contents

Foreword

Daisy King grew up on her grandparents' farm in Buford, Georgia, just outside sprawling metropolitan Atlanta. A truly classic southern woman, Miss Daisy is strong, resourceful, and in possession of many talents. Like all Southerners, she has adapted to the many changes that have reshaped the traditional values Southerners cherish.

Food, family, and entertaining at home with friends have long been components of the well documented southern lifestyle. Miss Daisy, however, is cutting a trail of new southern traditions based on an enlightened awareness of health and nutrition. Her Healthy Revelation may well be the road map for consumers who are aware of the basics of good nutrition and are looking for help in establishing a healthy nutritional lifestyle.

As the former owner of a chain of food stores in the South, I frequently was amazed at the degree to which some of my customers failed to recognize the relationship between the food they ate and a healthy body and mind. Many unwittingly became "food victims," thinking of food only in terms of how it tastes or relying on others to monitor the quality of what they eat. With all of the information available today, everyone should be able to take charge of their eating habits and enhance the value of the food they consume.

Miss Daisy's Healthy Southern Cooking will assist you in modifying your food choices and the methods you use to prepare traditional southern food. She puts her healthy spin on traditional southern recipes, utilizing pure foods with quick, simple preparation —"keeping the taste and losing the fat," as she calls it. These natural methods of preparation, coupled with thoughtful questions, will enable you to enjoy all the rituals surrounding food and the health benefits they offer.

Steven E. Crook
Former President and Owner,
Steven's Fun Fresh Food Stores

Acknowledgments

Thanks to the following people at Baptist Hospital in Nashville, Tennessee, for their contributions to this book: Lisa Sheehan-Smith, M.Ed., R.D., L.D.N.; Teri Briley, R.D., L.D.N.; DeeAnna Carney, R.D., L.D.N.; Marj Moore, R.D., L.D.N.; Barbara Pierce; Susan Santry, R.D., L.D.N.; Jenny Scidmore, R.D.; Chrystie Villines Turner, R.D., L.D.N., C.D.E.; Teresa Young; and Gina Smith.

Gratitude goes to Steven Crook, owner of Steven's Fun Fresh Food Stores until 1997, who allowed me to test recipes in the store's kitchens. Steven also provided an open door to visit with the daily consumers and discuss their nutritional needs.

Much appreciation to the people who requested Miss Daisy's Tea Room recipes reformatted for their dietary needs. Their inspiration keeps me updating and developing recipes for future enjoyment.

Introduction

As I look back over the years, it sometimes seems as if circumstances have gently brought me to where I could write *Miss Daisy's Healthy Southern Cooking*, which, at this point in my life, has been the most natural and reasonable thing I could have done. My varied experiences have given me special reasons to want to share with you a healthier way to enjoy southern food.

My parents died when I was very young, so my maternal grandparents raised me on their small working farm outside Atlanta. There we grew vegetables and froze them, made jelly and preserves, collected nuts from pecan trees, milked cows, gathered fresh eggs daily, cured country hams, and planted flowers.

While I was but a youngster, my grandmother taught me to prepare traditional southern foods using the products grown on our farm. She also taught me how to adapt recipes so that my grandfather could enjoy them. He was a diabetic and constantly had to control his consumption of sugars, carbohydrates, and fats. I learned a great deal about healthy eating during those years.

When I entered college, I intended to study journalism, foreign languages, and communications—anything that would prepare me for a career in traveling or speaking. On a whim one day I decided to obtain a double major—home economics and education—with a minor in speech and communication.

My first job after graduating from Belmont College in Nashville, Tennessee, was teaching home economics in a Catholic girls school. My assignment was to teach the students about nutrition, how to cook from recipes, and how to develop menus. Soon I found I enjoyed creating recipes and menus for the class to prepare. Some of the girls had fat-restricted diets or suffered from diabetes, and they needed recipes suitable for their needs. Twenty years ago there were fewer cookbooks on the market than are available today, so I had to reformulate many recipes for my students with special needs. For me, this experience emphasized the practical consequences of healthy eating.

I opened my first restaurant, Miss Daisy's Tea Room, in the fall of 1974 as an extension of my love for cooking and teaching. Many of the restaurant's guests had special dietary requests, and I found it a rewarding challenge to adjust my southern recipes to meet their needs. In her vegetable and flower gardens, Marilyn Lehew, my partner, grew many of the ingredients used in the dishes we served, and we used some of these fresh herbs in the special diet recipes, replacing much of the fat in many popular southern dishes with healthy flavor.

Recipes from Miss Daisy's, my first cookbook, was written as a result of my customers' requests for recipes for the food they enjoyed at Miss Daisy's Tea Room. Shortly after the book's publication, I was a guest on a television program in Chicago, discussing southern restaurants and recipes. As I was preparing one of the recipes from the cookbook, the show's hostess bluntly asked, "Why do southern recipes contain so much fat?" I quickly gave her a brief history of southern foods and southern cooking, and then I explained how many of the recipes can be enhanced with substitutions and by healthier cooking methods and techniques. In chapter 4 of this book I have provided examples for you.

For many years Helen Corbitt—cookbook author, dietician, and longtime proprietor of the Zodiac Room in the Neiman-Marcus stores—also inspired my ideas about cooking. She introduced me to the concept of spa cuisine in her *Greenhouse Cookbook,* and she was devoted to serving the purest foods with style and flourish. She regularly sent me recipes to try in my restaurants and encouraged me to compile a healthy lifestyle cookbook someday.

Miss Daisy's Creamed Chicken over Cornbread was a popular dish at the restaurant. The late Alex Haley, the noted author, loved this entrée. A diabetic, he knew his diet had to be controlled, and so he would save his carbohydrates for that special dish. I promised him that someday I would convert Creamed Chicken over Cornbread to a tasty low-fat version. The newly revised recipe is included in this book on page 169. I have kept my promise to my dear friend.

Year after year, guests who patronized Miss Daisy's requested low-fat, low-cholesterol, and low-calorie menus. During the seventeen years in which I operated the restaurant, I continued to develop, collect, and file recipes for a southern low-fat cookbook. When the restaurant chapter of my life closed in 1991, I began to compile the manuscript for this cookbook. I also extended my career in home economics into other food-related fields.

After closing Miss Daisy's, I joined Steven's, A Fun Fresh Food Store, in Nashville as the staff home economist. In this capacity I worked with store patrons, helping them plan menus and advising them about what to serve at parties, receptions, and special holiday events. I also had the opportunity to develop many recipes for Steven's kitchens, particularly for consumers who wanted delicious, satisfying, low-fat recipes, not just for special health reasons but as a lifestyle choice. Once again, I pulled out my collection of low-fat, high-fiber recipes.

I had begun a rough draft on this book when, in January 1993, my husband, Wayne, suddenly became seriously ill. After several weeks of testing, he underwent two major surgeries. Cancer, which we had thought he had licked, had recurred.

After successful surgeries, Wayne's doctor informed us that he would be a diabetic for the rest of his life. When the hospital nutritionist briefed us on his new diet choices, I shared with her my background as a home economist. I knew that I could help control his diabetes by planning and preparing his meals. In this way he would be able to eat with moderation all the foods he had enjoyed during our marriage. So my low-fat cookbook quickly took on another dimension: diabetic exchanges, which I have included with the nutritional information for each recipe in this book. Watching Wayne enjoy his favorite foods gave me yet another reason for completing this cookbook. (You can also find extensive information about the Diabetic Exchange Program in the Appendix, p. 263.)

Wayne was able to enjoy traditional foods with the exchanges I included in this book for five years. As a family we began to eat the low sugar, low carb, and low-fat foods that are required in the diet of a diabetic. Wayne's cancer continued to advance and three months before he passed away, February 20, 1998, he had to take insulin shots. He was so thankful that I wrote a cookbook not just for him but for the thousands of you who have been enlightened by the original publication.

I am very pleased with *Miss Daisy's Healthy Southern Cooking*. My greatest satisfaction is that I have provided you with recipes that are southern in taste, but which lack the characteristic fat and cholesterol of this style of cooking and meet the dietary needs of people with restricted diets.

My life has provided me with a wide variety of rich, meaningful experiences. Because of my interests in southern cooking and healthy living, these experiences have opened doors to a healthy lifestyle I might have missed otherwise.

This book is filled with ways to help you fine-tune a healthy lifestyle. It contains carefully developed and tested recipes for lighter, healthier foods that really taste good. The helpful grocery lists include the ingredients required for each recipe. The section on eating out will help you to make better choices when you're away from home, and the information on interpreting the new food product labels will make you a more informed consumer. I hope this book will prompt you to pursue a healthy lifestyle.

Daisy King

Miss Daisy's
HEALTHY SOUTHERN COOKING

Part One

THE HEALTHY REVELATION

1

THE HEALTHY LIFESTYLE

Today the word "lifestyle" is used frequently. It encompasses a wide variety of things, including family life, work, stress, social events, exercise, hobbies, fitness, diet, and daily habits.

We have all heard about the effects a stressful lifestyle can have on your health, and most people are aware of the relationship between their diet and their health. But many people do not realize that it is not necessary to feel like you are making a sacrifice to improve your diet and maintain your health.

If you read the paper, watch the news, or read books and magazines, you have no doubt discovered that a healthy diet may reduce your risk of heart disease, cancer, stroke, diabetes, and high blood pressure, not to mention help you maintain a healthy weight. And you may have already heard the good news that introducing a healthier lifestyle may even reverse some of the effects of an unhealthy diet.

There are so many books and articles on the subject of diet that it seems almost too difficult to take in, but in fact the principles are quite simple. Whether you are trying to stay healthy, lose weight, or control your diet at the instruction of a medical professional, you do not have to become an extremist.

Following are seven dietary guidelines that provide sound advice for healthy Americans ages two years and over.

- Eat a variety of foods
- Maintain a healthy weight
- Choose a diet low in fat, saturated fat, and cholesterol
- Choose a diet with plenty of vegetables, fruits, and grain products
- Use sugars only in moderation
- Use salt and sodium only in moderation
- If you drink alcoholic beverages, do so in moderation

To incorporate this advice into your daily food habits, here are some healthful tips on how to follow each guideline. It's as simple as . . .

EAT A VARIETY OF FOODS

Did you know that your body needs over forty different nutrients to stay healthy? Protein, carbohydrates, fat, vitamins, and minerals are all essential—yet no single food supplies you with all these nutrients in the necessary amounts. However, by using the Food Guide Pyramid to help you plan daily food choices you will obtain all of the nutrients needed and in the right amounts.

The pyramid is a general guide of what to eat each day, not a rigid prescription or diet. It calls for eating a variety of foods to provide you with the nutrients you need and enough calories to maintain a healthy weight.

A GUIDE TO DAILY FOOD CHOICES

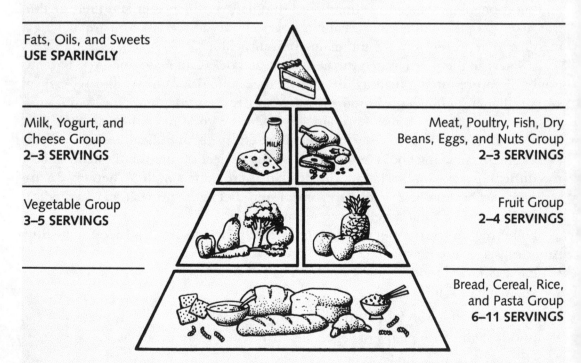

Fats, Oils, and Sweets
USE SPARINGLY

Milk, Yogurt, and
Cheese Group
2–3 SERVINGS

Meat, Poultry, Fish, Dry
Beans, Eggs, and Nuts Group
2–3 SERVINGS

Vegetable Group
3–5 SERVINGS

Fruit Group
2–4 SERVINGS

Bread, Cereal, Rice,
and Pasta Group
6–11 SERVINGS

FOOD GROUP	PORTION
Bread, Cereal, Rice, and Pasta	1 slice bread 1 ounce ready-to-eat cereal ½ cup cooked cereal, rice, pasta
Fruit	1 medium piece of fresh fruit ½ cup fresh, cooked, or canned fruit ¾ cup fruit juice
Vegetable	1 cup raw leafy vegetables ½ cup other vegetables ¾ cup vegetable juice
Meat, Poultry, Fish, Dry Beans, Eggs, and Nuts	2 to 3 ounces cooked lean meat, poultry, or fish ½ cup cooked dry beans, 1 egg, or 2 tablespoons peanut butter count as 1 ounce meat
Milk, Yogurt, and Cheese	1 cup milk or yogurt 1½ ounces natural cheese or 2 ounces processed cheese

MAINTAIN A HEALTHY WEIGHT

Did you know that your chances of developing a health problem are increased if you are too fat or too thin? The risk for high blood pressure, heart disease, stroke, diabetes, and certain types of cancer is greater when you are overweight. On the other hand, underweight women are at greater risk for osteoporosis, and both men and women who are underweight are at greater risk for premature death.

How do you establish your healthy weight? A quick glance at the chart on the next page will give you a good guideline.

SUGGESTED WEIGHTS FOR ADULTS

Height (without shoes)	Weight in pounds (without clothes)	
	19 to 34 years	35 years and over
5'0"	*97–128	108-138
5'1"	101–132	111-143
5'2"	104–137	115-148
5'3"	107–141	119-152
5'4"	111–146	122-157
5'5"	114–150	126-162
5'6"	118–155	130-167
5'7"	121–160	134-172
5'8"	125–164	138–178
5'9"	129–169	142–183
5'10"	132–174	146–188
5'11"	136–179	151–194
6'0"	140–184	155–199
6'1"	144–189	159–209
6'2"	148–195	164–210
6'3"	152–200	168–216
6'4"	156–205	173–222
6'5"	160–211	177–228
6'6"	164–216	182–234

* The higher weights in the ranges generally apply to men, who tend to have more muscle and bone; the lower weights more often apply to women, who have less muscle and bone.
Source: Derived from National Research Council, 1989–2000

If you find yourself tipping the scale, take a realistic approach! A slow weight loss of ½ to 1 pound per week is best—you will be losing body fat then instead of muscle. Try a 3-step approach:

1. Begin by selecting nutritious and delicious foods. Use the Food Guide Pyramid to help you choose the correct number of servings from each food group and the right portion size. Increase your fiber intake while decreasing your fat intake. (Read on to find tips on increasing fiber and decreasing fat intake.)

2. Include regular aerobic exercise (walking, cycling, swimming, jogging, aerobic dance) in your lifestyle. Your goal should be 3 to 5 times per week and 20 to 60 minutes per session. Don't overdo it initially; add more days and more time as you feel capable. "No pain, no gain" is OUT!

3. Develop some behavioral strategies: Keep a record of your eating habits; discover the situations that "trigger" you to eat, then remove the triggers; set realistic goals.

CHOOSE A DIET LOW IN FAT, SATURATED FAT, AND CHOLESTEROL

Almost everyone these days has heard that they need to eat less fat and cholesterol, but why? A high fat diet increases the risk for heart disease, certain types of cancer, stroke, and obesity. To reduce the risk for these lifestyle-related diseases, most health organizations, including the American Heart Association, recommend that no more than 30 percent of daily calories come from fat and to limit dietary cholesterol intake to 300 milligrams daily.

WHAT IS YOUR FAT BUDGET?

$$\frac{\text{Total Daily Calories} \times .30}{9 \text{ calories/gram}^*} = \text{Daily Fat Budget (grams)}$$

Example: A woman who consumes 1800 calories per day.

$$\frac{1800 \text{ calories} \times .30}{9 \text{ calories/gram}} = \frac{540 \text{ calories from fat}}{9 \text{ calories/gram}} = 60 \text{ grams}$$

*1 gram of fat contains 9 calories.

TYPES OF FAT

Saturated fat should provide no more than 10 percent of your daily calories. This type of fat is solid at room temperature and tends to raise blood cholesterol levels. Sources of saturated fat include:

- Meat
- Whole-milk dairy products
- Tropical oils (coconut oil, palm oil, palm kernel oil)
- Hydrogenated fats (stick margarine, vegetable shortenings)
- Cocoa butter
- Lard
- Beef tallow

Unsaturated fat comes in two varieties, polyunsaturated and monounsaturated. These fats are liquid at room temperature and tend to lower blood cholesterol levels. They should provide no more than 10 percent of your daily calories. Polyunsaturated fats are found in the following vegetable oils:

- Safflower oil
- Sunflower oil
- Corn oil
- Soybean oil
- Cottonseed oil

Monounsaturated fat may be the most beneficial fat for lowering blood cholesterol levels, and should provide 10 to 15 percent of your daily calories. This type of fat is found in olive and canola oils.

Cholesterol is only found in animal products such as meat, dairy products, and eggs. By eating less total fat and saturated fat you will also decrease your cholesterol intake.

Here are some tips to help you decrease the fat, saturated fat, and cholesterol in your diet.

- Limit meats (lean beef and pork, wild game, chicken, turkey, and seafood) to 6 ounces (cooked weight) per day. Choose seafood, skinless chicken, and turkey most often. Trim all visible fat from meats.
- Roast meats on a rack so fat can drip off and be discarded.
- Limit fats used in baking, cooking, and at the table to 5 to 8 teaspoons per day. Recommended fats include vegetable oils and soft (tub) margarines. Choose a margarine with "liquid" vegetable oil listed as the first ingredient. Avoid using meat fat, lard, or shortening for cooking.
- Avoid fried foods.
- Have at least one meatless meal per week. Try using dried beans or peas instead of meat.
- Use low-fat or nonfat dairy products. Cheese should have no more than 6 grams of fat per ounce.
- Use no more than 3 to 4 egg yolks per week, including those cooked in foods.
- Limit cream sauces, cheese sauce, and gravy unless prepared from a low-fat recipe. Make hot fruit sauces with no oil. Thicken by adding cornstarch to a cool fruit juice mixture and cook until thickened and boiling. Fruit sauces are delicious with desserts or over meat or fish.

- Try using low-fat or nonfat mayonnaise and salad dressings. Over fruit salad, use nonfat vanilla or fruit yogurt rather than mayonnaise or whipping cream.
- Eat pretzels, non-oil tortilla chips, or plain popcorn instead of regular chips and nuts.
- Choose low-fat or nonfat frozen yogurt, sherbet, or sorbet instead of ice cream.
- Gelatin, graham crackers, vanilla wafers, ginger snaps, fig bars, angel food cake, and hard candy are low-fat sweet alternatives.
- Eat more fruits, vegetables, and whole grain breads. They not only provide less fat, but an added bonus of more fiber.
- Always check labels on foods for the amount of fat and saturated fat per serving. Don't let the words "light" or "cholesterol free" fool you. These foods may still be high in fat.
- Check grams of fat on cereal boxes. Some that seem "healthy," such as granola cereals, are high in fat and sugar.
- Reduce the fat in cheese spreads by mixing with an equal amount of low-fat cottage cheese in a blender. It will reduce the fat by nearly half.
- Make tuna and chicken salads with nonfat mayonnaise or nonfat yogurt. Or try gradually diluting mayonnaise with the nonfat version, until you become accustomed to it.
- Sauté vegetables in a nonstick pan with a small amount of water or nonstick cooking spray. If sticking occurs, add water and steam until the water is gone, watching to make sure the vegetables do not burn. If possible, do not add any grease when browning meat.
- Top baked potatoes with nonfat sour cream, low-fat yogurt, or low-fat cottage cheese.
- When browning meat, especially ground meat, drain off the fat and turn the meat onto a paper-towel-lined plate to absorb more grease. Blot cooked patties with paper towels, too.
- Most of the fat in fruit pies is in the crust. You can reduce fat calories by not eating the crust, and by making fruit pies without crusts.
- When possible, use cocoa powder instead of baking chocolate in recipes. It is much lower in fat, especially saturated fat. (Baking chocolate is made with cocoa butter, one of the highly saturated fats.)

CHOOSE A DIET WITH PLENTY OF VEGETABLES, FRUITS, AND GRAIN PRODUCTS

The purpose of this guideline is to encourage us to eat a diet rich in fiber—or roughage, as Grandma called it. There are many reasons to eat a high-fiber diet, including:

- Prevention and management of constipation, hemorrhoids, and diverticular disease.
- Protective benefits against certain types of cancer.
- Lower cholesterol levels.
- Help in stabilizing blood sugar levels in persons with diabetes.
- Vital nutrients such as complex carbohydrates, vitamins, and minerals.

The American Dietetic Association recommends 20 to 35 grams of fiber per day. This can be achieved by following the guidelines of the Food Guide Pyramid, which encourages greater consumption of foods from the Bread, Cereal, Rice, and Pasta groups, as well as Fruits, Vegetables, and Legumes (dried beans and peas). Here are some tips to help you increase fiber in your diet.

- Eat whole fruits instead of and besides drinking fruit juices.
- Serve fruit on cereals at breakfast.
- Try whole grain rice. Add brown or wild rice to white rice dishes.
- Eat the peels of fruits and potatoes.
- Consider fruit for dessert. It is great with nonfat vanilla or fruit flavored yogurt as a topping, and it makes a great accompaniment for ice milk and nonfat frozen yogurt.
- Add raisins, dried fruits, or shredded vegetables (carrots, sweet potatoes, and zucchini, for example) to muffins and spice cakes.
- Add lettuce, tomatoes, and sprouts to sandwiches. (They make a great sandwich together, too.)
- Snack on popcorn and raw vegetables. Keep peeled and ready-to-eat vegetables in the refrigerator.
- Have bean or vegetable soup as an appetizer.
- Eat high-fiber cereal for breakfast. (Be sure to check the labels, because some "health" cereals are high in fat.)
- Try whole wheat bread instead of white bread. There are even whole wheat varieties of English muffins and waffles now.

- Have dried beans instead of meat for the main dish. Substitute black beans, kidney beans, and garbanzo beans for some or all of the meat in stir-fry and casserole recipes.

- Substitute whole wheat flour for a third of the all-purpose flour in breads and many cake recipes.

- Try mixing whole wheat pasta with regular pasta. You may gradually switch completely to whole wheat pasta.

Following is a chart showing the grams of fiber in fruits, cooked and raw vegetables, legumes, breads, pastas, flours, nuts, seeds, and breakfast cereals.

FOOD	AMOUNT	GRAMS OF DIETARY FIBER
fruits		
apple (w/skin)	1 medium	3.5
banana	1 medium	2.4
cantaloupe	¼ melon	1.0
cherries, sweet	10	1.2
peach (w/skin)	1	1.9
pear (w/skin)	½ large	3.1
prunes	3	3.0
raisins	¼ cup	3.1
raspberries	½ cup	3.1
strawberries	1 cup	3.0
orange	1 medium	2.6
vegetables, cooked		
asparagus, cut	½ cup	1.0
beans, string or green	½ cup	1.6
broccoli	½ cup	2.2
brussels sprouts	½ cup	2.3
parsnips	½ cup	2.7
potato (w/skin)	1 medium	2.5
spinach	½ cup	2.1
sweet potato	½ medium	1.7
turnip	½ cup	1.6
zucchini	½ cup	1.8
vegetables, raw		
celery, diced	½ cup	1.1
cucumber	½ cup	0.4
lettuce, sliced	1 cup	0.9
mushrooms, slices	½ cup	0.9
tomato	1 medium	1.5
spinach	1 cup	1.2

FOOD	AMOUNT	GRAMS OF DIETARY FIBER
legumes		
baked beans	½ cup	8.8
dried peas, cooked	½ cup	4.7
kidney beans, cooked	½ cup	7.3
lima beans, cooked	½ cup	4.5
lentils, cooked	½ cup	3.7
navy beans, cooked	½ cup	6.0
breads, pasta, and flours		
bagels	1 bagel	0.6
bran muffins	1 muffin	2.5
French bread	1 slice	0.7
oatmeal bread	1 slice	0.5
pumpernickel bread	1 slice	1.0
whole wheat bread	1 slice	1.4
rice, brown, cooked	½ cup	1.0
spaghetti, cooked	½ cup	1.1
nuts and seeds		
almonds	10 nuts	1.1
peanuts	10 nuts	1.4
popcorn, popped	1 cup	1.0
breakfast cereals		
All-Bran	⅓ cup	8.5
Bran Buds	⅓ cup	7.9
Bran Chex	⅔ cup	4.6
Bran Flakes	¾ cup	4.0
Raisin Bran-type	¾ cup	4.0
shredded wheat	⅔ cup	2.6
oatmeal, regular, quick, and instant, cooked	⅔ cup	1.6
cornflakes	1¼ cup	0.3

Source: *Fiber Facts,* American Dietetic Association

USE SUGARS ONLY IN MODERATION

Sugars and foods that are mostly sugar are often high in calories yet low in nutrients. Therefore, they provide little added benefit to a nutritious diet. This may not be a concern for someone who is following the Food Guide Pyramid recommendations, exercising regularly, and maintaining a healthy weight. An overweight person or a person with diabetes, however, would need to avoid eating large amounts of sugar in order to control calories. For people with diabetes, concentrated carbohydrates (sugars, sweets, etc.) are released into the bloodstream quickly, causing a rapid rise in glucose levels. As a result, the disease is more difficult to manage when sugar is consumed.

Table sugar (sucrose) is only one form of sugar. Other words to be aware of are:

- Brown sugar
- Corn syrup
- Dextrin
- Dextrose
- Fructose
- Raw sugar
- Sorghum
- Galactose
- Glucose
- Honey
- Invert sugar
- Lactose
- Sorbitol
- Fruit juice concentrate
- Maltose
- Mannitol
- Mannose
- Maple Syrup
- Molasses
- Xylitol

Try to limit foods that have any of the above as a primary ingredient (one of the first two in a list of ingredients) or foods that have several of the above listed as ingredients. None of them need to be avoided completely. Sometimes they're necessary in small amounts to make a recipe successful.

Noncaloric sweeteners are alternative sweeteners for those trying to reduce sugar in their diet. Noncaloric sweeteners are much sweeter than table sugar (sucrose).

COMMON SWEETENERS				
Common Name	Sweetener	Amount	Calories	Sugar Equivalent
Table Sugar	Sucrose	1 tsp	16	1 tsp
Sweet 'N Low	Saccharin	1 packet	4	2 tsp
Sugar Twin	Saccharin	1 packet	6	2 tsp
Sweet One	Acesulfane-K	1 packet	4	2 tsp
Equal or Nutrasweet*	Aspartame	1 packet	4	2 tsp
Splenda	Sucralose	1 tsp	0	1 tsp

*Aspartame cannot be used for baking as exposure to heat for long periods of time will cause loss of sweetness.

So what is moderation? Use sugar and foods high in sugar sparingly. Try to eat those foods *dense* in nutrients first and then, health permitting, just a little bit! Here are some tips to help you reduce the sugar in your diet.

- Reduce the sugar in recipes by one fourth. When you become accustomed to the taste, try reducing it by another quarter. This will cause baked goods to be more dense, but it will not destroy the flavor.

- Use fruit-only preserves and spreads, and sugar-free or low-sugar jams and jellies.
- When you crave sweets, substitute fruits. Keep fewer candy and dessert items in your cabinets.
- Serve unsweetened cereals with fresh or dried fruits.
- Buy frozen and canned fruits with little or no sugar added.
- Add seltzer or club soda to unsweetened fruit juices for an interesting drink.

USE SALT AND SODIUM ONLY IN MODERATION

Sodium is essential for our bodies. It helps muscles and nerves to function properly and also helps to maintain the body's water balance. However, too much sodium can act like a sponge and cause extra water to remain in your body. This can put a burden on your heart and place more pressure on your blood vessels.

The average American consumes about 4,000 to 6,000 milligrams of sodium daily, yet our bodies only need approximately 1,100 to 3,300 milligrams per day. Sodium is found in most of our foods and it occurs naturally in some foods. However, the major source of sodium in our diet is added salt. Salt is 40 percent sodium, containing over 2,000 milligrams of sodium per teaspoon.

Since excessive amounts of sodium can be a health risk, the following table lists some suggestions for lowering your sodium intake.

Fresh Is Best	Much of the sodium we consume is added during the processing of our foods.
Taste Foods	Don't automatically add salt to foods before tasting them.
Experiment	Try alternative herbs and spices.
Read Labels	Know what you are eating.
Avoid Obviously Salty Snacks	Try a low sodium alternative.

Here are some tips to help you reduce the sodium in your diet.

- Reduce the salt you add in cooking by half. Or decrease by one fourth, and after about a month, reduce it by another quarter. Most people do not notice the difference. Soon the dish will taste too salty when prepared with your usual amount of salt.
- Use lite salt, which will reduce the sodium by half.

- Remove the salt shaker from the table. Use herbs and spices in place of salt. Some great substitutes are garlic powder, onion powder, lemon pepper, lemon juice, vinegar, chili sauce, and Tabasco sauce.
- Eat natural foods rather than processed foods.
- Check the labels on cereals. They can be high in sodium.
- Combine an equal amount of no-salt-added tomatoes to spaghetti sauce. This will cut the sodium in half.
- Do not add salt to the water for boiling pastas or hot cereals.
- Rinse canned beans and tuna for one minute in running water.
- Double the amount of water called for when preparing canned soups. Add sliced carrots, diced potatoes, and pasta to soups.

IF YOU DRINK ALCOHOLIC BEVERAGES, DO SO IN MODERATION

Alcoholic beverages provide calories yet few nutrients to our diets. Besides contributing no health benefits, drinking alcoholic beverages can:

- be linked to many health problems such as certain cancers and liver disease.
- harm the growing fetus during pregnancy.
- contribute to accidents involving dangerous equipment or while driving.
- interact with medications.

Some studies have shown that moderate alcohol intake can protect us against heart disease; however, many experts agree that there are healthier and safer ways to decrease the risk for heart disease such as through diet, exercise, and not smoking.

What is moderation?

- Men: No more than 2 drinks a day
- Women: No more than 1 drink a day

What is a drink?

- 12 ounces of regular beer
- 4 to 5 ounces of wine
- 1½ ounces of distilled beverages (80 proof), i.e., whiskey, vodka, etc.

~ 2 ~

DINING OUT

$\mathcal{D}$ining out is no longer reserved for weekends or special occasions. It has become a way of life. Selecting nutritious foods from restaurant menus has become easier over recent years.

Many restaurants include light, healthy, or spa cuisine selections in their menus. A picture of an apple is often used to denote "heart healthy" items.

If you are going to dine out, plan ahead. Eat sensibly, but cut back on your other meals during the day. Try to walk an extra mile at your lunch break or add an extra workout to burn more calories. If you know that dinner will be served late in the evening, eat a light snack before you leave home. Raw vegetables, fruits, or fat-free crackers are suggestions that will help you contain your hunger.

Once you are seated for dinner, ask your waiter how a dish is prepared. Is it boiled, baked, poached, or roasted? If the dish is not fried, it will usually meet the fat restrictions. Ask questions about any additional fat used in preparing the dish. It is fine to ask your server to request the chef's assistance in preparing a dish to satisfy your dietary needs.

SUGGESTION GUIDE FOR NUTRITIOUS FOODS WHEN DINING OUT

1. Request that salad dressings, butter, margarine, mayonnaise, and sour cream be served separately on a side dish. Use lemon juice or vinegar for a dressing or bring your own low-calorie dressing from home.
2. Order clear soups like broths or consommé, or vegetable-based soups such as gazpacho, instead of cream soups.
3. Specify that no fat should be added to whatever type of chicken, fish, or red meat you order.

4. Ask that your sandwiches be served without mayonnaise or margarine on the bread. Chicken, turkey, low-fat cheeses, and lean meats are recommended fillings.

5. Remove all visible fat from poultry or meat.

6. Try to avoid bean salads, tuna salads, chicken salads, pasta salads, and potato salads made with mayonnaise. Choose a lettuce salad, plain vegetables, or sliced tomatoes.

7. Choose vegetables served without sauce or added butter or margarine.

8. Avoid rich muffins, sweet rolls, and breads. Choose plain breads or rolls and low-fat crackers such as soda crackers, rye crackers, or Melba toast. Use margarine or butter sparingly.

9. Order entrées or appetizers that are broiled, steamed, roasted, poached, or stir-fried.

10. Watch portion sizes; if it's more than you should eat, ask for a "doggy bag."

11. Order a main course of healthy appetizers to keep portion sizes manageable.

12. Choose entrées made with vegetables and grains, and side dishes such as curries, pilafs, or stir-fry; avoid fried rice.

13. Choose fresh fruit, fruit ices, low-fat frozen yogurt, sorbet, or angel food cake for a low-fat dessert.

14. Learn to recognize words on the menu that indicate when low-fat preparation techniques have been used. Such techniques include steaming, grilling, broiling, and poaching.

Fast-Food Choices

Fast-food restaurants are a way of life in the United States. The main advantage to this type of food is that it is fast, easy, and convenient. One nutritional advantage is that the meals are high in protein, but there are many disadvantages unless you choose wisely. Surprisingly however, there are more healthful selections available than ever before, and the choices are increasing every day.

Sometimes, if you are faced with eating at a fast-food restaurant and don't care for the menu, there is an alternative. Some restaurants will let you buy everything that goes on a sandwich à la carte. Some food chains will let you substitute fruit for French fries. It never hurts to ask. Being a former restaurant owner, I can attest to this form of help. All restaurants are aware of the growing desire for nutritional foods and strive to accommodate consumers' needs.

The supermarket is another choice for a complete fast-food meal. Several supermarkets have developed so-called "marketplace" stores. These stores are large fresh food centers with a vast array of prepared food options such as ethnic kitchens, fruit and vegetable bars, salads prepared to order, sushi bars, and the continually updated product assortment in the deli department.

Today the consumer has the opportunity to purchase many healthful items produced by the supermarket deli. Chicken is being fried in lower cholesterol oil, barbecued with lighter sauces, and prepared skinless in the most popular way—roasted. Pizzas are available now with lower fat and lower cholesterol ingredients. Many varieties of seafood, chicken, and vegetables are prepared to order or packaged for reheating. You may select a grab-and-go sandwich on breads such as pitas, bagels, and cracker breads filled with your favorite sliced deli meats, veggies, and low-fat chicken or tuna salads.

The greatest revelation in the supermarket deli is the offering of hot and refrigerated items to go. Entrées, side dishes, and salads, to name a few, are ready for you to take to the office or your dining table at home.

Eating Out the Low-Fat Way

More people eat away from home than ever before. But the thought of dining out when trying to eat healthy or lose weight usually brings an attitude of defeat even before you get out of the house or away from the office. *Where to go . . . , what to eat . . . , salad again . . . , why bother, there's nothing I can eat anyway. . . .* These are some of the things that may cross your mind. In today's society, even though many people choose a diet high in fat and cholesterol, restaurants are beginning to offer choices (some of them very good ones). All you have to do is know what to look for and where to look.

Make the right choices so you can dine out without feeling deprived and remain on your healthy plan. If you normally follow a healthy eating plan, sometimes you may feel the need to splurge and order something that may not be recommended. That's okay sometimes, as long as you don't make it a weekly habit.

Remember, just because you splurge (let's say for example that you'd like to have a hamburger for dinner), you don't have to "blow it" totally. Have your hamburger (leave off the mayonnaise) and instead of French fries, have a baked potato using your low-fat substitutions. Or perhaps you'd like a luscious dessert: often once you've tasted it, you'll find that all you really wanted was one or two bites anyway. Try sharing the dessert with friends, or ask the waiter for a small portion if you are by yourself. Better yet, treat everyone to nonfat yogurt on the way home.

Visualize dining out as an adventure and look at all the things that you can have instead of focusing on all the things you shouldn't have.

3

THE SUPERMARKET

Supermarkets offer nutrition information programs to demonstrate their commitment to meeting consumers' interest in health and nutrition. This is done through advertisements and promotions, food labels, and product information at point-of-purchase.

The supermarket has been described as a vehicle for change. These changes reflect not only trends in health promotions and regulations but other trends in marketing, communications, education, and evaluation. Major concern is directed toward foods sold, health promotion programs used, and consistent labels.

In the last decade there has been increasing agreement on the role food choices play in the risk of developing heart disease, some types of cancer, and other diet-related diseases. Dietary recommendations emphasize reducing the amount of certain nutrients such as fat, carbohydrates, cholesterol, sodium, and calories.

This emphasis still exists. Programs, however, are beginning to emphasize the benefits of positive food choices: vegetables, fruits, whole grain foods, fish, poultry, lean meats, and low-fat dairy products. Under new government regulations, food manufacturers will be allowed to make health claims on their products for the first time.

Today, health promotion programs such as the "5 a Day for Better Health" program and "Project Lean" (Low-fat Eating for America Now) offer partnerships between government and/or a professional health organization and the supermarket.

Labeling has been confusing in the past due to the inconsistency in program criteria. But the label laws instituted in 1994 give the consumer a more consistent description of the product. The Nutrition Labeling and Education Act (NLEA) mandated consistent nutritional labeling on most packaged and processed foods. In addition, the NLEA established voluntary guidelines for the supermarket to provide nutrition information at point-of-purchase for fresh produce, raw seafood, meat, and poultry.

FACTS ON FOOD LABELING

Previously, the nutrition information found on food labels was voluntary unless a nutrient had been added or a nutrition claim had been made. Now the information is required by the government. Here is an example of the mandated nutritional information label.

But what do the claims really mean? Claims such as "light" or "low-fat" can only be used if the food meets the government definition of that claim.

FOOD LABELS

Reading the nutritional label provides you with the information you need about the food you are buying or eating. What you see on the food label—the nutrition and ingredient information—is required by the government. Numbers on the nutrition label may be rounded for labeling.

Serving Size
Similar food products have similar serving sizes. This makes it easier to compare foods. Serving sizes are based on amounts people actually eat.

Label Information
The nutrient list covers those nutrients most important to your health.

Vitamins and Minerals
Only two vitamins, A and C, and two minerals, calcium and iron, are required on the food label. A food company can voluntarily list other vitamins and minerals in the food.

Nutrition Facts

Serving Size 1 cup (228g)
Servings Per Container 2

Amount Per Serving

Calories 90	Calories from Fat 30

	% Daily Value*
Total Fat 3g	5%
Saturated Fat 0g	0%
Cholesterol 0mg	0%
Sodium 300mg	13%
Total Carbohydrate 13g	4%
Dietary Fiber 3g	12%
Sugars 3g	
Protein 3g	

Vitamin A 80%	•	Vitamin C 60%
Calcium 4%	•	Iron 4%

* Percent Daily Values are based on a 2,000 calorie diet. Your daily values may be higher or lower depending on your calorie needs:

		Calories:	2,000	2,500
Total Fat	Less than		65g	80g
Sat Fat	Less than		20g	25g
Cholesterol	Less than		300mg	300mg
Sodium	Less than		2,400mg	2,400mg
Total Carbohydrate			300g	375g
Dietary Fiber			25g	30g

Calories per gram:
Fat 9 • Carbohydrate 4 • Protein 4

Percent Daily Value
PercentDaily Value shows how a food fits into a 2,000-calorie reference diet. You can use Percent Daily Value to compare foods and see how the amount of a nutrient in a serving of food fits into a 2,000-calorie reference diet.

Daily Value Footnote
Daily Values are the reference numbers. These numbers are set by the government and are based on current nutrition recommendations. Some labels list the daily values for a daily diet of 2,000 and 2,500 calories. Your own nutrient needs may be less than or more than the Daily Values on the label.

Calories Per Gram Footnote
Some labels tell the approximate number of calories in a gram of fat, carbohydrate, and protein.

LABEL CLAIM	DEFINITION*
Calorie Free	Less than 5 calories
Low Calorie	40 calories or less**
Light or Lite	⅓ fewer calories or 50% less fat; if more than half of the calories are from fat, fat content must be reduced by 50% or more
Light in Sodium	50% less sodium
Fat Free	Less than ½ gram fat
Low-fat	3 grams or less fat**
Cholesterol Free	Less than 2 milligrams cholesterol and 2 grams or less saturated fat**
Low Cholesterol	20 milligrams or less cholesterol and 2 grams or less saturated fat**
Sodium Free	Less than 5 milligrams sodium**
Very Low Sodium	35 milligrams or less sodium**
Low Sodium	140 milligrams or less sodium**
High Fiber	5 grams or more fiber

*Per Reference Amount (standard serving size). Some claims have higher nutrient levels for main dish products and meal products, such as frozen entrées and dinners.
**Also per 50 g for products with small serving sizes (Reference amount is 30 g or less or 2 tbsp or less).

Health claims about the relationships between a nutrient or a food and the risk of disease are another feature on the label. The following claims are allowed:

- Calcium and Osteoporosis
- Fat and cancer
- Saturated fat and cholesterol and coronary heart disease
- Fiber-containing grain products, fruits, vegetables, and cancer
- Fruits, vegetables, and grain products that contain fiber and risk of coronary heart disease
- Sodium and hypertension (high blood pressure)
- Fruits and vegetables and cancer

How to Find Your Own Nutrient Needs

Daily Values are the reference numbers on the food label. These numbers are based on current nutrition recommendations. The Percent Daily Values on the food label are based on a 2,000-calorie reference diet.

If you don't eat 2,000 calories a day, you may want to know your own nutrient needs for fat, saturated fat, carbohydrate, fiber, and protein. Amounts for these nutrients can be estimated for your own calorie level using current nutrition recommendations. The Daily Values for cholesterol, sodium, vitamins, and minerals stay the same for all calorie levels. You can use your personal nutrient amounts to build a healthful diet.

YOUR DAILY CALORIE LEVEL

Women

Age	Low Activity	Moderate Activity	High Activity
19–24	1,800	2,200	2,600
24–50	1,800	2,200	2,600
51+	1,700	2,000	2,400

Men

Age	Low Activity	Moderate Activity	High Activity
19–24	2,300	3,000	3,700
24–50	2,300	3,000	3,800
51+	2,000	2,600	3,200

Source: Calorie levels derived from the Recommended Dietary Allowances, 10th edition. National Research Council, pp. 29, 33.

Your Own Nutrient Needs

The Daily Values on the nutrition label are only reference amounts. It's important to find your own nutrient needs that match your calorie level. The chart on the next page will help you pinpoint your nutrient needs.

How to Use Percent Daily Value

You can use Percent Daily Value to compare foods quickly and see how the amount of a nutrient in a serving of food fits in a 2,000 calorie reference diet. For example,

NUTRIENT NEEDS FOR DIFFERENT CALORIE LEVELS*

Food Component	Calories					
	1,600	2,000**	2,200	2,500	2,800	3,200
Total Fat (g)	53	65	73	80	93	107
Saturated Fat (g)	18	20	24	25	31	36
Total Carbohydrate (g)	240	300	330	375	420	480
Dietary Fiber (g)	20***	25	25	30	32	37
Protein (g)	46****	50	55	65	70	80
Total % Daily Value for each of these nutrients can add up to:	80%	100%	110%	125%	140%	160%

*Numbers may be rounded.
**Percent Daily Value on the label for total fat, saturated fat, carbohydrate, dietary fiber, and protein (if listed) is based on a 2,000 calorie reference diet.
***20 g is the minimum amount of fiber recommended for all calorie levels below 2,000.
Source: National Cancer Institute.
****46 g is the minimum amount of protein recommended for all calorie levels below 1,800.
Source: Recommended Dietary Allowances.
Note: These calorie levels may not apply to children and adolescents, who have varying caloric requirements.

you can use Percent Daily Value to see how much dietary fiber is in a serving of food compared to other food products and compared to a 2,000 calorie reference diet.

You can also use Percent Daily Value to see if your diet fits within current nutrition recommendations. Let's say you eat 2,000 calories a day. If your total Percent Daily Value for dietary fiber in all the foods you eat in one day adds up to 100 percent, your diet fits within the recommendations for fiber. Likewise, if the total Percent Daily Value for fat in all the foods you eat in one day adds up to 100 percent or less, your diet fits within the recommendations for fat.

You can add Percent Daily Value for any calorie level. If you eat 1,600 calories, your total Percent Daily Value for a single nutrient (fat, saturated fat, carbohydrate, fiber, or protein) in all the foods you eat in one day can add up to 80 percent. If you eat 2,800 calories, your total Percent Daily Value for each nutrient in all the foods you eat in one day can add up to 140 percent.

SHOPPING GUIDE

Spices and Baking Products
All-purpose Flour
Almond Extract
Bacon Soy Bits
Baking Soda
Baking Powder
Basil, Dried
Bay Leaves
Black Peppercorns
Black Pepper, Ground
Brown Sugar Substitute
Cake Flour
Canola Oil
Celery Seed
Chili Powder
Cilantro, Dried
Cinnamon, Ground
Cloves, Ground
Coriander
Cornflake Crumbs
Cornstarch
Cream of Tartar
Cumin
Curry Powder
Dill, Dried
Dry Mustard
Durkee's Sauce
Garlic Powder
Granulated sugar
Ground Red Pepper
Ground White Pepper
Ground Ginger
Honey
Italian Herb Seasoning
Kitchen Bouquet
Lemon Extract
Low-Calorie Cooking
  Spray
Marjoram, Dried
Molasses

Molly McButter
Nonfat Dry Milk
Non-stick Cooking Spray
Nutmeg
Olive Oil
Onion Flakes, Dried
Onion Powder
Oregano, Dried
Paprika
Parsley Flakes
Polenta
Poppy Seeds
Poultry Seasoning
Powdered Sugar
Rosemary, Dried
Rum Extract
Safflower Oil
Salt Substitute
Salt, Lite
Savory
Sesame Seeds
Sugar Substitute, all
  varieties
Tabasco Sauce
Taco Seasoning
Tarragon, Dried
Thyme, Dried
Unbleached Flour
Vanilla Extract
Vegetable Oil
Whole Wheat Flour
Yellow Cornmeal

Canned Seafood
Minced Clams
Red or Pink Salmon
Water-packed Tuna
White Crab Meat

Beverages
Sugar-free Soda Pop

Sugar-free Seltzer
Sugar-free Hot Cocoa Mix
Apple Juice
Grape Juice
Herbal Teas
Crystal Light

*Canned and Packaged
Products, Miscellaneous*
Almonds
Bean Sprouts
Chinese Style Vegetables
Dates
Dried Beef
Dried Green Chilies
Dry Sherry
Enchilada Sauce
Low-sodium Soy Sauce
Pecans
Pine Nuts
Popcorn, low-fat
Raisins
Reduced Fat Peanut
Butter
Refried Beans
Salsa
Sugar-free Vanilla Instant
  Pudding
Sugar-free Chocolate
  Instant Pudding
Sugar-free Gelatin, all
  flavors
Sun-dried Tomatoes
Unflavored Gelatin
Unsalted Pretzels
Walnuts
Water Chestnuts
Whole Green Chilies

Dressings, Sauces, Vinegars, and Jams
- Au Jus Gravy Mix
- Chili Sauce
- Dijon Mustard
- Catsup
- Low-calorie Salad Dressing
- Low-fat Mayonnaise
- Low-sugar Jams
- Low-sugar Marmalade
- Miracle Whip, Lite
- Mustard Mayonnaise
- No-sugar Fruit Spreads
- Nonfat Mayonnaise
- Picanté Sauce
- Pickle Relish
- Raspberry Vinegar
- Red Wine Vinegar
- Reduced-calorie Mayonnaise
- Rice Vinegar
- Salsa
- Spaghetti Sauce
- Vinegar
- Worcestershire Sauce

Canned Vegetables (Use no salt added, if available)
- Artichoke Hearts
- Black Beans
- Canned Tomatoes
- Creamed Corn
- Garbanzo Beans
- Green Beans
- Kidney Beans
- Mushrooms
- Pinto Beans
- Split Peas
- Stewed Tomatoes
- Tomato Paste
- Tomato Sauce
- Vegetarian Baked Beans

Whole Kernel Corn

Canned Fruit (Use no sugar added, if available)
- Apple Juice
- Apricots
- Canned Pumpkin
- Cherry Pie Filling, Lite
- Crushed Pineapple
- Lemon Juice
- Lime Juice
- Mandarin Oranges
- Peaches
- Pears
- Pineapple Slices
- Pineapple Juice
- Pineapple Chunks
- Unsweetened Applesauce
- Wholeberry Cranberry Sauce

Pasta (eggless), Dried Beans, Grains
- Angel Hair Pasta
- Barley
- Black Beans, Dried
- Brown Rice
- Bulgur
- Dried Couscous
- Fettucine Noodles
- Fusilli Pasta
- Kidney Beans, Dried
- Lasagna Noodles
- Lentils
- Lima Beans, Dried
- Linguine Noodles
- Macaroni, Elbow
- Orzo
- Pinto Beans, Dried
- Quick Cooking Oats
- Red Beans, Dried
- Regular Oats
- Spaghetti Noodles
- White Beans, Dried

White Rice

Frozen Foods
- Bread Dough
- Broccoli, Cauliflower, Carrots in Cheese Sauce
- Chicken Breasts
- Chopped Spinach
- Cooked Shrimp
- Fish Fillets, Sole, Snapper, Salmon
- Frozen Berries and Fruits (no sugar added)
- Green Peas
- Ground Turkey
- Ground Beef, low-fat
- Orange Juice Concentrate
- Oriental-style Vegetables
- Pea Pods
- Phylo Dough
- Reduced-fat Vegetables
- Turkey Breasts

Soups: Low-fat, Low-sodium
- Any desired low-fat, low-sodium
- Beef Broth
- Chicken Broth
- Cream of Celery
- Cream of Chicken
- Tomato Soup
- Vegetable Broth

Cereals, Breads, Crackers, Treats
- 100% Bran
- All Bran
- All Fruit Sweetened Cookies
- All Fat-free Cookies
- Bagels
- Bran Buds
- Chocolate Thin Wafers
- English Muffins

Fat-free Fig Bars
Fat-Free Snack Cakes
Gingersnaps
Graham Crackers
Grape Nuts
Melba Toast
Oat bran
Quick Cooking Oatmeal
Rice Cakes
Ry-Krisps
Special K
Unsalted Saltines
Vanilla Wafers
Whole Grain Cereals (less than 3 grams of fat per serving)

PERISHABLES

Herbs/Spices (Fresh)
Basil
Chives
Cilantro
Dill
Ginger
Mint
Oregano
Parsley
Sage
Thyme

Fresh Fruit
Apples
Bananas
Blueberries
Grapes
Lemons
Limes
Melons
Oranges
Peaches
Pineapples

Breads
Bagels
Corn Tortillas
English Muffins
Flour Tortillas
Focaccia Bread
French Rolls
French Bread
Hamburger Buns
Pita Breads
Whole Wheat

Fresh Vegetables
Asparagus
Cabbage
Carrots
Cucumber
Green Beans
Green Bell Peppers
Leeks
Lettuce
Mushrooms
Okra
Onions
Red Bell Peppers
Squash (all)
Tomatoes (all)
Yellow Bell Peppers

Meat, Poultry, Seafood
Clams
Deli Meats, low-fat and sliced
Eye of Round Roast
Flank Steak
Fresh Chicken Breasts
Fresh Turkey Breasts
Ground Turkey
Leg of Lamb
Round Steak, whole and ground
Salmon
Sea Scallops
Shrimp
Sole
Tenderloin
Top Sirloin Steak
Whitefish

~~4~~

RECIPE PREPARATION

*A*fter you have finished your grocery shopping, you will be ready to begin preparation of the recipes. Assemble all of the ingredients and utensils. Make sure the equipment needed is in working order. Some recipes require preheating the oven.

The ingredients are listed in the order they are used. Some ingredients are converted products from traditional ones. The method of their incorporation into the recipe may be different from recipes you have previously prepared. Be sure to read the entire recipe before you begin preparation.

Using the recipes in this book can be your first step toward making a lifestyle change. Eating well does not mean you have to deprive yourself of your favorite dishes. The recipes in this book are designed to show you just how delicious and satisfying nutritious eating can be. They are low in fat, carbohydrates, cholesterol, sodium, and calories, and high in fiber. The recipes have been modified to use creative cooking techniques and ingredient substitutions, but without sacrificing taste.

Some cooking techniques are better than others for cutting fat, calories, and cholesterol while enhancing the flavor and nutritional value of foods. As you prepare the recipes you will see that many of the following techniques are used:

COOKING METHODS

Baking This method cooks food in an oven with dry heat. Oven-frying is a low-fat baking technique in which food bakes on a rack (so all sides will be equally exposed to the heat).

Braising Browning food, usually large cuts of meat and then cooking tightly covered in a small amount of liquid at low heat for a long period of time.

Broiling	Food cooked directly under the heat source.
Grilling	The product is placed on a metal or ceramic grid above the heat source. The fat drips away from the food onto the heat source, creating a smoke which helps flavor the food. Many new stove tops come with a grill top. There are also many products on the market for indoor grilling, such as stovetop grill pans and two-sided electric grilling machines.
Poaching	Poached foods cook in water or broth that is held just below the boiling point. This method is excellent for fish and poultry.
Roasting	This method bakes food at a moderate temperature to produce a well-browned exterior and moist interior.
Sautéing	This form of cooking is best done in a sauté pan or non-stick skillet. It cooks food quickly in a small amount of liquid.
Steaming	Foods cooked over boiling water. This may be done by using double pans or a separate steamer.
Stir-Frying	Cooking food over high heat while stirring constantly. A large heavy skillet or wok may be used.

To change an ingredient is somewhat more complicated. The recipe must be analyzed to see where modification could be made without changing the basic structure of the finished product. The recipes were tested using a fat-free, lower fat, lower sodium or reduced calorie product. Most of the higher fat recipes were reduced. Any high fat or sugar ingredient that could be eliminated was. A great help now is the availability of alternative ingredients found on supermarket shelves.

The following substitution list is a sampling of alternative ingredients to make recipes more healthful.

RECIPE LISTING	USE INSTEAD
American, Cheddar, Swiss, or Monterey Jack cheese	Cheese with 5 grams of fat or less per ounce
Jarlsberg	Jarlsberg lite
Boursin	Boursin lite
Mozzarella	Part skim mozzarella
Cream cheese	Fat-free cream cheese Neufchâtel cheese or light cream cheese

Ricotta	Part skim, nonfat or lite ricotta
Sour cream	Nonfat or low-fat sour cream or nonfat or low-fat yogurt
Whole or 2% milk	Skim milk, 1% milk, or nonfat dry milk mixed with water
Milk shakes	Frozen yogurt shake or one made from nonfat milk, fruit, and ice
Whipping cream	Chilled evaporated skimmed milk, whipped Whipped Topping Recipe found on p. 253
Half and half	Half evaporated skim milk plus half skim milk
1 whole egg	2 egg whites or ¼ cup egg substitute
2 egg yolks	¼ cup Egg Beaters per yolk
Margarine or butter	Reduced-calorie margarine, fat-free mayonnaise, unsweetened applesauce with fat-free mayonnaise
Vegetable oil	Reduce amount, using a polyunsaturated or monounsaturated oil
Cooking oil for frying	Pam non-stick cooking spray, Butter Buds for basting or coating foods
Mayonnaise	Nonfat, reduced-calorie, or low cholesterol mayonnaise
Gravy	Gravy made with bouillon granules or broth and thickened with cornstarch
Condensed cream soups or canned soups	Broth or brand name low-fat, low-sodium canned soups
White flour, 1 cup	½ cup whole wheat plus ½ cup white flour
Salt	Reduce by half or eliminate by using lots of herbs and spices or salt-free substitutes
Sugar	For every cup, ½ cup frozen fruit juice concentrate or sugar substitutes
Pastry and pie crusts	Phyllo dough in supermarket freezer section and pie crust recipes in this book
1 ounce unsweetened or semisweet chocolate	3 tablespoons dry cocoa powder plus 2 tablespoons Butter Buds liquid
Coconut	Coconut extract
Egg noodles	Eggless noodles
White rice	Brown or wild rice
Nuts	Reduce by half or use Grape-Nuts cereal
Salad dressings	Fat-free salad dressings
Prepared breadcrumbs	Whole wheat breadcrumbs

- *Peas:* Anise and onion powder; rosemary and marjoram
- *Potatoes:* Dill, onion powder, and parsley; caraway seeds and onion powder; nutmeg and chives; rosemary, sage, sesame seeds, and thyme
- *Spinach:* Curry powder and ginger; nutmeg and garlic; basil
- *Squash:* Mint and parsley; tarragon and garlic; allspice and basil
- *Tomatoes:* Basil and rosemary; oregano

RECIPE ANALYSIS

The nutritive values that concern us most are calories, carbohydrates, fat, sodium, and fiber. The recipes in this book were analyzed according to a computerized nutrient analysis program by the nutrition staff of Baptist Hospital in Nashville, Tennessee. Lisa Sheehan-Smith and her staff compiled a program to analyze every available nutrient. A sample of the data provided by this program is included in this section.

To determine whether your recipes need to be altered to fit your new lifestyle, you may accumulate the nutritional data for the ingredients in the recipe, and determine its appropriateness. To calculate your own recipe, you must collect information from the labels on packages and cans of food, and the nutritive values of meats, produce, and dairy. I would suggest starting a file of your own.

Once you have determined that a recipe needs altering, the substitution ingredient list on pages 32–34 and the tips in Chapter 1 are a helpful way to start adjusting recipes of your own. Start by reducing the sugar, fat, or sodium. Your recipe may have to undergo several taste tests and recalculations before you come up with a satisfying dish, but do not give up.

The chart on the next page is a simple way to help you analyze recipes you already use or new ones you collect.

Recipe Name _____

Date Tested _____

Equipment Used _____

Temperature _____

Cooking or Baking Time _____

Number of Servings _____

Comments _____

Ingredient	Amount	Calories	Fat	Carbohydrates	Sodium	Cholesterol	Fiber
Total Nutritive Values							
Divide by Number of Servings							
Round to Nearest Number							

Part Two

THE RECIPES

5

MENUS

New Year's Day Supper

STRAWBERRY SPINACH SALAD
Page 114
ROASTED PORK TENDERLOIN
Page 157
SPICY HOT BLACK-EYED PEAS

TURNIP SOUFFLÉ
BUTTERMILK CORN MUFFINS
Page 145
APPLE CRISP
Page 258

SPICY HOT BLACK-EYED PEAS

1   *medium yellow onion, chopped*
½   *green bell pepper, chopped*
1   *17-ounce can black-eyed peas*
1   *16-ounce can no-salt-added whole tomatoes,*
     undrained and chopped
1   *teaspoon dry mustard*
½   *teaspoon chili powder*
½   *teaspoon liquid smoke*
1   *teaspoon soy sauce*
1   *teaspoon minced fresh parsley*

Assemble all ingredients and utensils. Coat a large saucepan with vegetable spray and sauté the onion and bell pepper. In a saucepan combine the remaining ingredients except the parsley and heat to boiling. Reduce the heat and simmer for 20 minutes. Pour the mixture into a 2-quart casserole dish and sprinkle with parsley. Yields 8 servings of ½ cup each.

Calories: 62; Fat: 0.5g; Cholesterol: 0 mg; Sodium: 194 mg; Carbohydrates: 11 g; Fiber: 1 g; Diabetic Exchange: 1 vegetable, ½ starch

TURNIP SOUFFLÉ

1   *tablespoon reduced-calorie margarine*
1   *tablespoon all-purpose flour*
½   *cup low-fat milk*
⅛   *teaspoon salt*
2   *cups cooked mashed turnips*
½   *cup egg substitute, well beaten*
2   *egg whites, stiffly beaten*
    Grated nutmeg

Assemble all ingredients and utensils. Preheat the oven to 375°. Coat a 1½-quart casserole dish with vegetable spray. In a large saucepan melt the margarine and blend in the flour. Gradually add the milk, then season with salt. Cook, stirring constantly, until thickened. Add the turnips and cool slightly. Add the egg substitute and fold in the egg whites. Spoon the mixture into the prepared dish. Place the dish in a larger pan of hot water. Bake at 375° for 30 minutes or until set. Sprinkle lightly with grated nutmeg. Yields 6 servings.

Calories: 60; Fat: 2 g; Cholesterol: 0.2 mg; Sodium: 158 mg; Carbohydrates: 5.98 g; Fiber: 0.9g; Diabetic Exchange: 2 vegetable

Directors' Luncheon

CHICKEN CRÊPES WITH RED PEPPER SAUCE	CHOCOLATE MOUSSE PIE *Page 236*
FRUIT SALAD WITH POPPY SEED DRESSING *Page 135*	COFFEE OR TEA

CHICKEN CRÊPES WITH RED PEPPER SAUCE

3   *tablespoons reduced-calorie margarine, divided*
½   *cup sliced fresh mushrooms*
1   *cup diced cooked chicken breast*
¼   *cup low-fat sour cream*
1   *tablespoon minced fresh parsley*
¼   *teaspoon ground black pepper*
½   *10-ounce package frozen spinach, cooked and well drained*
     Crêpes (recipe follows)
     Red Pepper Sauce (see recipe, p. 219)

Assemble all ingredients and utensils. Preheat the oven to 425°. In a saucepan melt the margarine and sauté the mushrooms. Remove the pan from the heat. Mix in the chicken, sour cream, parsley, black pepper, and spinach. Fill 8 of the crêpes with an equal amount of mixture. Arrange the crêpes in a baking pan. Bake at 425° for 15 minutes. Serve with Red Pepper Sauce. Yields enough filling for 8 crêpes.

Calories: 64; Fat: 4g; Cholesterol: 15 mg; Sodium: 51 mg;
Carbohydrates: 2g; Fiber: 0.3g; Diabetic Exchange: 1 lean meat

CRÊPES

½   cup cold water
½   cup cold nonfat milk
1   egg plus 2 egg whites
¼   teaspoon salt
1   cup all-purpose flour
1   tablespoon safflower oil

Assemble all ingredients and utensils. In a blender or food processor combine the water, milk, egg, egg whites, and salt. Blend until mixed, then add the flour, then the oil. Blend on high, scraping down the sides of the blender. Cover and refrigerate for 2 hours.

Heat a 6-inch nonstick frying pan over moderately high heat. When the pan is hot, pour in ¼ cup of batter and immediately rotate the pan until the batter covers the bottom. Cook until light brown. Turn and brown the other side. Slide onto a warm plate and repeat for each crepe. Yields 10 to 12 crêpes.

Calories: 66; Fat: 2g; Cholesterol: 25 mg; Sodium: 70 mg; Carbohydrates: 9g; Fiber: 0 g; Diabetic Exchange: 1 starch

---

Wedding Brunch

FRESHLY SQUEEZED ORANGE JUICE	CRANBERRY FREEZE *Page 251*
CRAB MORNAY OVER ENGLISH MUFFINS	CHOCOLATE OATMEAL CAKE COFFEE OR TEA

CRAB MORNAY

Serve over English muffins.

4 *green onions, chopped*
1 *cup chopped fresh mushrooms*
2 *tablespoons water*
½ *cup low-fat milk*
2 *teaspoons cornstarch*
2 *ounces low-fat Swiss cheese, grated*
1 *cup fresh crab meat or drained and flaked canned crab meat*

Assemble all ingredients and utensils. In a large skillet sauté the green onions and mushrooms in the water until soft. Set the vegetables aside. In a saucepan combine the milk and cornstarch, mixing well. Cook until heated through. Stir in the vegetables, cooking until the sauce is thickened. Add the cheese and crab, gently stirring until the cheese is melted. Yields 2 cups or 16 servings of 2 tablespoons each.

Calories: 30; Fat: 0.9g; Cholesterol: 9 mg; Sodium: 165 mg; Carbohydrates: 1 g; Fiber: 0 g; Diabetic Exchange: ½ lean meat

CHOCOLATE OATMEAL CAKE

½   cup safflower oil

⅓   cup honey

1   large egg

½   cup rolled oats

1   cup whole-wheat flour

1   tablespoon baking powder

½   cup semisweet chocolate chips

¾   cup low-fat milk

Assemble all ingredients and utensils. Preheat the oven to 350°. Spray an 8-inch square pan with vegetable spray.

In a large mixing bowl cream together the oil, honey, and egg. Add the oats, flour, baking powder, chocolate chips, and milk. Mix until blended. Pour the batter into the prepared pan. Bake at 350° for 35 to 40 minutes or until the cake tests done. Yields 12 2-inch squares.

Calories: 205; Fat: 13g; Cholesterol: 23g; Sodium: 122 mg; Carbohydrates: 22g; Fiber: 0.6g; Diabetic Exchange: 1½ starch, 2 fat

Southern Breakfast

COMPOTE OF MELON BALLS	BUTTERMILK BISCUITS
BREAKFAST SCRAMBLE	*Page 148*
HERBED TOMATOES	BLACKBERRY FRUIT SPREAD
MISS DAISY'S GARLIC	COFFEE OR TEA
CHEESE GRITS	
Page 202	

BREAKFAST SCRAMBLE

½   cup low-fat cottage cheese
1   tablespoon reduced-calorie margarine
1   tablespoon all-purpose flour
½   cup low-fat milk
1   cup frozen egg substitute, thawed (equivalent to 4 eggs)
2   tablespoons minced fresh chives
1   tablespoon finely chopped red bell pepper

Assemble all ingredients and utensils. In a food processor purée the cottage cheese until smooth. Set it aside.

In a heavy saucepan melt the margarine and blend in the flour. Cook for 1 minute. Slowly add the milk, stirring constantly until thickened. Set the pan aside. In a large nonstick skillet cook the egg substitute, stirring frequently, until set. Gently stir in the cottage cheese, white sauce mixture, chives, and red pepper. Cook until the mixture is firm but moist. Yields 4 servings.

Calories: 102; Fat: 4g; Cholesterol: 2 mg; Sodium: 255 mg;
Carbohydrates: 3 g; Fiber: 0.2 g; Diabetic Exchange: 2 lean meat

HERBED TOMATOES

From my cookbook *Gracious Entertaining, Southern Style.*

3 large ripe tomatoes
½ teaspoon salt
¼ teaspoon ground black pepper
⅓ cup finely minced parsley
⅓ cup finely minced chives
2 tablespoons safflower oil
⅓ cup tarragon vinegar

Assemble all ingredients and utensils. Peel the tomatoes and cut them crosswise in half. Place the tomatoes in a deep bowl, sprinkling each half with seasonings and herbs. Combine the oil and vinegar and pour the mixture over the tomatoes. Cover and chill for an hour or more, basting often. To serve, drain the dressing and arrange the tomatoes on a platter. Yields 6 servings.

Calories: 59; Fat: 5g; Cholesterol: 0 mg; Sodium: 186 mg;
Carbohydrates: 5g; Fiber: 0.7 g; Diabetic Exchange: 1 vegetable, 1 fat

Summer Bridge Luncheon

TURKEY PASTA SALAD	RAISIN BRAN MUFFINS
CONGEALED ORANGE	*Page 147*
CARROT SALAD	COFFEE OR TEA
Page 114	

TURKEY PASTA SALAD

6   *ounces seashell macaroni, uncooked*
¾   *pound cooked low-fat turkey breast, cubed*
2   *cups diced tomato*
½   *cup diced celery*
¼   *cup minced red onion*
¼   *cup chopped fresh parsley*
2   *tablespoons red wine vinegar*
1   *tablespoon vegetable oil*
1   *tablespoon grated Parmesan cheese*
2   *teaspoons dried dill*
1   *clove garlic, minced*
½   *teaspoon freshly ground pepper*

Assemble all ingredients and utensils. Cook the pasta according to the package directions. Drain, rinse under cold water, and drain again. In a large bowl combine the cooked pasta, turkey, tomato, celery, onion, and parsley. Mix well. In a separate bowl combine the vinegar and the remaining ingredients. Pour the vinegar mixture over the pasta mixture, and toss gently to combine. Cover and refrigerate for 2 hours or more. Yields 8 servings of 1 cup each.

Calories: 157; Fat: 3 g; Cholesterol: 18 mg; Sodium: 625 mg; Carbohydrates: 19.32 g; Fiber: 0.5g; Diabetic Exchange: 1 lean meat, 1 starch, 1 fat

Sunday Lunch

TENDERLOIN POT ROAST

MUSHROOM BARLEY CASSEROLE
Page 201

SQUASH MEDLEY

FRESH FRUIT WITH
POPPY SEED DRESSING
Page 135

DILL BREAD
Page 152

YUMMY CHOCOLATE CAKE
Page 233

COFFEE OR TEA

TENDERLOIN POT ROAST

1   *3-pound beef tenderloin roast*
¼   *cup soy sauce*
1   *tablespoon Worcestershire sauce*
1   *clove garlic, crushed*
2   *onions, quartered*
½   *pound fresh mushrooms, sliced*
3   *ribs celery, sliced*
3   *carrots, peeled and sliced*
¼   *cup water*
4   *to 6 small new potatoes, halved*

Assemble all ingredients and utensils. Place the tenderloin in a bowl. In a small bowl combine the soy sauce, Worcestershire sauce, and garlic. Pour the mixture over the tenderloin and marinate overnight.

Preheat the oven to 325°. In a roasting pot place the marinated tenderloin, onions, mushrooms, celery, and carrots. Cover. Bake at 325° for 2 hours and 30 minutes.

Add the potatoes and water, and bake for another 30 minutes. Yields 12 servings of 3 ounces of tenderloin plus divided vegetables per person.

Calories: 230; Fat: 10 g; Cholesterol: 73 mg; Sodium: 363 mg; Carbohydrates: 10 g; Fiber: 0.5g; Diabetic Exchange: 3 lean meat, ½ starch

SQUASH MEDLEY

1   *tablespoon safflower oil*
2   *cups chopped zucchini*
2   *cups chopped summer squash*
2   *cups chopped gooseneck yellow squash*
1   *medium onion, chopped*
¼   *teaspoon dried dill*
¼   *teaspoon ground black pepper*

Assemble all ingredients and utensils. In a large sauté pan heat the oil and sauté the remaining ingredients until tender but crisp. Yields 8 servings of ½ cup each.

Calories: 38; Fat: 2g; Cholesterol: 0 mg; Sodium: 3 mg; Carbohydrates: 5 g; Fiber: 1 g; Diabetic Exchange: 1 vegetable, ½ fat

Family Supper

MISS DAISY'S MEAT LOAF
Page 159

TOMATO ASPIC

SOUTHERN CORN PUDDING

FRESH STEAMED BROCCOLI

HERB CHEESE BREAD
Page 154

PEACH CRUMBLE
Page 246

COFFEE OR TEA

TOMATO ASPIC

2   *3-ounce packages sugar-free lemon gelatin*
1½ *cups boiling water*
2   *cups low-sodium tomato juice*
1   *bay leaf*
1   *cup chopped celery*
½   *cup chopped green onion*
½   *teaspoon ground black pepper*

Assemble all ingredients and utensils. In a mixing bowl dissolve the gelatin in boiling water. Add the remaining ingredients. Pour the mixture into 6 individual molds or an 8-inch square pan. Discard the bay leaf. Refrigerate until congealed. Yields 6 servings of ¾ cup each.

Calories: 30; Fat: 0.1 g; Cholesterol: 0 mg; Sodium: 115 mg; Carbohydrates: 5g; Fiber: 0.2g; Diabetic Exchange: 1 vegetable

SOUTHERN CORN PUDDING

½   cup chopped onion

½   cup chopped green bell pepper

⅓   cup chopped red bell pepper

2   tablespoons all-purpose flour

½   teaspoon ground cumin

¼   teaspoon chili powder

⅛   teaspoon salt

⅛   teaspoon ground black pepper

1   cup evaporated skim milk

¼   cup frozen egg substitute, thawed

3   cups fresh corn cut from the cob (about 5 ears)

Assemble all ingredients and utensils. Preheat the oven to 350°. Coat a large skillet with vegetable spray. Add the onion and chopped peppers, and sauté for 5 to 7 minutes or until tender. Add the flour, cumin, chili powder, salt, and pepper. Cook for 1 minute, stirring constantly. Gradually add the milk, stirring constantly until thickened and bubbly. Gradually stir about a fourth of the hot mixture into the egg substitute. Pour the egg substitute mixture into the saucepan, stirring constantly. Remove the pan from the heat and stir in the corn. Spoon the mixture into a 2-quart casserole dish. Bake at 350° for 45 minutes or until set. Yields 8 servings of ½ cup each.

Calories: 96; Fat: 1 g; Cholesterol: 1 mg; Sodium: 96 mg,
Carbohydrates: 18 g; Fiber: 1 g; Diabetic Exchange: 1 starch, ½ vegetable

Dinner Party

TURKEY PÂTÉ	STEAMED ASPARAGUS
Page 73	DILL NEW POTATOES
CHILLED MELON SOUP	*Page 213*
Page 96	CHOCOLATE MOUSSE PIE
BOSTON LETTUCE WITH	*Page 236*
VINAIGRETTE DRESSING	OR RASPBERRY BOMBE
POACHED FILLET OF SOLE	*Page 250*

BOSTON LETTUCE WITH VINAIGRETTE DRESSING

½   *cup balsamic vinegar*
2   *teapsoons fresh lemon juice*
1½ *cups safflower oil*
1   *teapoon Dijon mustard*
½   *teaspoon chopped fresh chives*
⅛   *teaspoon salt*
¼   *teaspoon freshly ground black pepper*
     Boston lettuce

Assemble all ingredients and utensils. In a small mixing bowl combine all of the ingredients except the lettuce. Beat with an electric mixer until well blended. Refrigerate until needed. Bring the dressing to room temperature. Divide the lettuce into servings. Toss each serving with 2 tablespoons of dressing. The dressing will keep up to a week in the refrigerator. Yields about 2 cups or 16 servings of 2 tablespoons each.

Calories: 91; Fat: 10 g; Cholesterol: 0 mg; Sodium: 13 mg;
Carbohydrates: 0 g; Fiber: 0 g; Diabetic Exchange: 2 fat

POACHED FILLET OF SOLE

2   *cups low-sodium, low-fat chicken broth*
¼   *cup lemon juice*
½   *teaspoon ground white pepper*
3   *bay leaves*
1   *teaspoon minced garlic*
3   *tablespoons dry sherry, optional*
2   *pounds sole fillets*

Assemble all ingredients and utensils. In a large skillet combine everything except the fish. Bring the mixture to a boil. Reduce the heat and
add the fish. Cover and simmer for 3 to 5 minutes depending on thickness, or until the fish flakes easily. Remove the fish with a slotted spatula.
Yields 8 servings of 4 ounces each.

Calories: 110; Fat: 1 g; Cholesterol: 54 mg; Sodium: 95 mg;
Carbohydrates: 1 g; Fiber: 0 g; Diabetic Exchange: 3 lower fat meat

Fourth of July Picnic

FRESH RAW VEGETABLE WITH
PARTY SPINACH DIP
Page 66

CRUNCHY BAKED CHICKEN
Page 170

FESTIVE CORN SALAD

CELEBRATION APPLE PIE

BASIL TOMATOES

STAR SPANGLED PUNCH

FESTIVE CORN SALAD

3   cups frozen whole kernel corn
2   4-ounce jars diced pimiento, drained
1   cup chopped green bell pepper
½   cup chopped green onions
1   tablespoon sugar substitute
¼   cup apple cider vinegar
2   teaspoons celery seeds
1   tablespoon safflower oil
½   teaspoon salt

Assemble all ingredients and utensils. Cook the corn according to the package directions, omitting salt. Drain and chill. In a serving bowl combine the corn, pimiento, and remaining ingredients, stirring well. Cover and chill the salad for at least 2 hours before serving. Yields 8 servings of ½ cup each.

Calories: 83; Fat: 2 g; Cholesterol: 0 mg; Sodium: 145 mg;
Carbohydrates: 17 mg; Fiber: 1 g; Diabetic Exchange: 1 starch

CELEBRATION APPLE PIE

$4\frac{1}{2}$ cups peeled, sliced apples
2   tablespoons lemon juice
$\frac{1}{2}$ cup sugar
2   tablespoons all-purpose flour
$\frac{1}{2}$ teaspoon cinnamon
$\frac{1}{4}$ teaspoon grated nutmeg
$\frac{1}{4}$ cup all-purpose flour
3   tablespoons brown sugar
1   tablespoon reduced-calorie margarine
$\frac{1}{8}$ teaspoon cinnamon
1   9-inch pastry crust

Assemble all ingredients and utensils. Preheat the oven to 325°. In a large bowl combine the apple slices and lemon juice. Toss gently to coat. In a separate bowl combine the sugar, 2 tablespoons of flour, ½ teaspoon of cinnamon, and nutmeg, and stir to blend. Sprinkle the mixture over the apples and toss gently to coat. Spoon the filling into the pastry crust. Set aside.

In a small bowl combine ¼ cup of flour, brown sugar, margarine, and ⅛ teaspoon of cinnamon. Stir well. Sprinkle the mixture evenly over the apple filling. Bake at 375° for 30 minutes. Decrease the oven temperature to 325° and bake for an additional 10 minutes or until the apples are tender. Yields 1 9-inch pie or 10 servings.

Calories: 188; Fat: 7 g; Cholesterol: 0 mg; Sodium: 65 mg;
Carbohydrates: 30 g; Fiber: 1 g; Diabetic Exchange: 1½ starch, ½ fruit, 1½ fat

BASIL TOMATOES

2   large tomatoes, sliced ¼-inch thick
½   teaspoon chopped fresh basil
1   teaspoon chopped garlic
¼   teaspoon salt
⅛   teaspoon black pepper

Assemble all ingredients and utensils. Arrange the tomatoes in a single layer on a baking sheet or platter. In a small bowl combine the basil, garlic, salt, and pepper. Spread the mixture evenly on top of the tomato slices. Cover and chill. Yields 4 servings of 2 tomato slices each.

Calories: 13; Fat: 0.2 g; Cholesterol: 0 mg; Sodium: 138 mg; Carbohydrates: 4 g; Fiber: 0.5 g; Diabetic Exchange: ½ vegetable

STAR-SPANGLED PUNCH

2   20-ounce packets unsweetened flavored soft drink mix
1   quart water
3   quarts chilled sugar-free ginger ale

Assemble all ingredients and utensils. Dissolve the drink mix in the water and chill. When ready to serve, add the chilled ginger ale. If using a punch bowl for serving, add a frozen fruit ice ring to float in the bowl. Yields 1 gallon or 32 servings of ½ cup each.

Calories: 3; Fat: 0 g; Cholesterol: 0 mg; Sodium: 33 mg; Carbohydrates: 0 g; Fiber: 0 g; Diabetic Exchange: free

Holiday Dinner

STEAMED ASPARAGUS WITH FRESH LEMON	SWEET POTATOES IN ORANGE CUPS
CRANBERRY RELISH *Page 111*	GINGERED YOGURT AMBROSIA *Page 253*
TURKEY BREAST WITH APPLE BREAD STUFFING	OR PUMPKIN MOUSSE PIE *Page 235*
	COFFEE OR TEA

APPLE BREAD STUFFING

4   *cups whole wheat breadcrumbs*
1   *cup chopped celery*
1   *cup chopped onion*
1   *tablespoon chopped fresh parsley*
1   *clove garlic, minced*
1   *cup defatted turkey or chicken broth*
2   *baking apples, peeled, cored, and diced*
¼   *teaspoon freshly ground black pepper*
½   *teaspoon ground sage*
½   *teaspoon minced fresh thyme*
¼   *teaspoon dried basil*

Assemble all ingredients and utensils. Preheat the oven to 350°. In a large bowl combine all of the ingredients and mix well. Spoon the batter into a 2-quart casserole dish. Bake at 350° for 40 to 45 minutes. Yields 8 servings of ½ cup each.

Calories: 47; Fat: 0.5 g; Cholesterol: 0 mg; Sodium: 68 mg; Carbohydrates: 10 g; Fiber: 2 g; Diabetic Exchange: ½ starch

SWEET POTATOES IN ORANGE CUPS

4   *medium sweet potatoes, unpeeled*
¼   *cup pineapple juice*
2   *tablespoons safflower oil*
1   *tablespoon crushed pineapple*
⅛   *teaspoon cinnamon*
⅛   *teaspoon nutmeg*
3   *large oranges, halved and contents removed*
     Orange slices or fresh mint for garnish

Assemble all ingredients and utensils. Preheat the oven to 375°. Spray a baking dish with nonstick cooking spray. In a large pot boil the potatoes until tender, about 30 minutes. Remove the skins. In a large mixing bowl mash the potatoes. Add the pineapple juice and oil, and whip until fluffy. Add the pineapple and spices. Fill each orange cup with the potato mixture and arrange the oranges in the prepared pan. Bake at 375° for 20 minutes or until lightly browned. Garnish with a fresh orange slice or fresh mint. Yields 6 servings of ½ cup each.

Calories: 163; Fat: 5 g; Cholesterol: 0 mg; Sodium: 14 mg; Carbohydrates: 28 g; Fiber: 0.9 g; Diabetic Exchange: 2 bread, 1 fat

6

APPETIZERS

MISS DAISY'S HOT ARTICHOKE SPREAD

1   cup low-fat cottage cheese
½   cup grated Parmesan cheese
2   tablespoons plain nonfat yogurt
2   tablespoons nonfat mayonnaise
¼   teaspoon hot sauce
1   clove garlic, minced
1   14-ounce can artichoke hearts, drained and finely chopped
    Melba rounds or toast points

Assemble all ingredients and utensils. Preheat the oven to 350°. Coat a
1-quart baking dish with vegetable spray. In a food processor or blender
combine all of the ingredients except the artichokes and bread. Mix until
smooth. Add the artichokes and stir to blend. Pour the mixture into the
prepared dish. Bake at 350° for 20 minutes. Serve hot. Yields 2 cups or 16
servings of 2 tablespoons each.

Calories: 32; Fat: 1 g; Cholesterol: 3 mg; Sodium: 130 mg;
Carbohydrates: 3 g; Fiber: 0.2 g; Diabetic Exchange: 1 vegetable

FRUITY DIP

Great in the center of a fresh fruit tray.

1⅓ cups vanilla low-fat yogurt
¼ cup low-sugar orange marmalade
⅓ teaspoon ground cinnamon

Assemble all ingredients and utensils. In a serving bowl combine all of the ingredients. Cover and refrigerate. Yields 1½ cups or 24 servings of 1 tablespoon each.

Calories: 15; Fat: 0.1 g; Cholesterol: 1 mg; Sodium: 8 mg;
Carbohydrates: 2 g; Fiber: 0 g; Diabetic Exchange: free

SALMON SPREAD

Serve with low-fat crackers or raw veggies.

1 12-ounce package light cream cheese
½ cup low-fat sour cream
1 teaspoon Worcestershire sauce
1 tablespoon lemon juice
⅛ teaspoon ground black pepper
½ teaspoon dill
2 tablespoons finely chopped green onion
1 15½-ounce can water-packed red salmon, drained (or 2 cups cooked and flaked fresh)

Assemble all ingredients and utensils. Soften the cream cheese. Remove the skin from the salmon and discard the large bones. Mash the splinter-type bones into the salmon. In a medium bowl blend the first 6 ingredients with an electric mixer. Stir in the onions and salmon. Transfer the dip to a serving bowl. Yields 2¾ to 3 cups or 2 tablespoons per serving.

Calories: 69; Fat: 5 g; Cholesterol: 20 mg; Sodium: 170 mg;
Carbohydrates: 1 g; Fiber: 0 g; Diabetic Exchange: 1 lower fat meat

SALMON DILL DIP

Great with any low-fat cracker.

1   cup low-fat cottage cheese
1   5-ounce can pink salmon with bones, drained
1   tablespoon minced green onion
1   teaspoon fresh lemon juice
2   tablespoons chopped dill pickles
⅛   teaspoon hot sauce
½   teaspoon ground black pepper

Assemble all ingredients and utensils. Remove the largest bones from the salmon. Mash the splinter-type bones. In a food processor or blender combine the cottage cheese and salmon, and process until smooth. Stir in the remaining ingredients. Transfer the mixture to a serving bowl. Yields 1½ cups or 12 servings of 2 tablespoons each.

Calories: 31; Fat: 1 g; Cholesterol: 7 mg; Sodium: 166 mg;
Carbohydrates: 1 g; Fiber: 0 g; Diabetic Exchange: ½ lower fat meat

CRAB DIP

4   ounces light cream cheese, softened

2   cups low-fat cottage cheese

3   tablespoons lemon juice

2   teaspoons prepared horseradish

¼   teaspoon Tabasco sauce

⅓   cup chopped green onion

1   6½-ounce can white crab meat, drained (or 6 ounces cooked fresh)

Assemble all ingredients and utensils. In a blender or food processor blend the cream cheese, cottage cheese, lemon juice, horseradish, and Tabasco sauce until smooth. Stir in the onion and crab meat. Transfer the dip to a serving dish. Yields 3 cups, or 24 servings of 2 tablespoons each.

Calories: 33; Fat: 1 g; Cholesterol: 11 mg; Sodium: 116 mg; Carbohydrates: 1 g; Fiber: 0 g; Diabetic Exchange: ½ lower fat meat

MEXICAN BEAN DIP

Great served with tortilla chips.

¼ *cup diced green chilies*
¼ *cup tomato sauce*
4 *green onions, minced*
½ *teaspoon ground cumin*
½ *clove garlic, minced*
1 *30-ounce can refried beans*

Assemble all ingredients and utensils. In a saucepan combine the chilies, tomato sauce, onions, and seasonings, and cook over medium heat for about 5 minutes. Add the beans and cook for another 5 minutes. Transfer the dip to a serving dish. Serve either hot or cold. Yields 4 cups or 16 servings of 4 tablespoons each.

Calories: 67; Fat: 1 g; Cholesterol: 0 mg; Sodium: 275 mg; Carbohydrates: 12 g; Fiber: 0.3 g; Diabetic Exchange: 1 starch

BEAN DIP

Great served with low-fat crackers or tortilla chips.

¾ *cup cooked kidney beans, drained*
2 *tablespoons picante sauce*
½ *teaspoon lime juice*

Assemble all ingredients and utensils. In a blender combine all of the ingredients and process until smooth. Transfer the dip to a serving dish. Chill. Yields ¾ cup or 14 servings of 1 tablespoon each.

Calories: 12; Fat: 0.6 g; Cholesterol: 0.2 mg; Sodium: 59 mg; Carbohydrates: 2 g; Fiber: 0 g; Diabetic Exchange: free

TOASTED ONION DIP

Great served with raw veggies.

3   tablespoons minced onion
1   cup nonfat yogurt
2   teaspoons low-sodium beef bouillon

Assemble all ingredients and utensils. Brown the minced onion on a baking sheet in a 400° oven for about 5 to 8 minutes. Cool. In a serving bowl combine all of the ingredients and mix well. Chill. Yields 1 cup or 16 servings of 1 tablespoon each.

Calories: 10; Fat: 0.1 g; Cholesterol: 0.2 mg; Sodium: 12 mg; Carbohydrates: 2 g; Fiber: 0.2 g; Diabetic Exchange: free

PARTY SPINACH DIP

Great served with raw veggies.

1   10-ounce package frozen chopped spinach
¼   package (2 tablespoons) dry vegetable soup mix
1½ cups plain nonfat yogurt
½   cup reduced-calorie mayonnaise
1   8-ounce can water chestnuts, drained and chopped
2   tablespoons chopped green onion
⅛   teaspoon dry mustard

Assemble all ingredients and utensils. Thaw the spinach, drain, and squeeze until dry. In a serving bowl combine the remaining ingredients. Yields 4 cups or 32 servings of 2 tablespoons each.

Calories: 23; Fat: 1 g; Cholesterol: 2 mg; Sodium: 68 mg; Carbohydrates: 2 g; Fiber: 0.1 g; Diabetic Exchange: free

ALTERNATIVE SOUR CREAM

Add fresh dill or chives to make a dip.

½ cup skim milk
2 cups low-fat cottage cheese

Assemble all ingredients and utensils. In a blender combine the milk and cottage cheese. Blend until smooth. Transfer the mixture to a serving dish or storage container. Yields 2¼ to 2½ cups or 28 servings of 2 tablespoons each.

> Calories: 20; Fat: 0.1 g; Cholesterol: 1 mg; Sodium: 100 mg;
> Carbohydrates: 1 g; Fiber: 0 g; Diabetic Exchange: free

CHILI CON QUESO

Great with nonfat tortilla chips.

3 green onions, chopped
1 clove garlic, minced
3 tablespoons water
1 8-ounce can stewed tomatoes, drained
1 4-ounce can chopped green chilies, drained
¼ teaspoon cayenne pepper
1 cup freshly grated low-fat Monterey Jack cheese

Assemble all ingredients and utensils. In a saucepan sauté the onions and garlic in water until soft, approximately 8 minutes. Add the chilies, tomatoes, and cayenne pepper. Cook over low heat for another 8 to 10 minutes, stirring often. Add the cheese and stir until melted. Transfer the dip to a serving dish. Yields 2 cups or 8 servings of 4 tablespoons each.

> Calories: 52; Fat: 3 g; Cholesterol: 8 mg; Sodium: 219 mg;
> Carbohydrates: 3 g; Fiber: 0.3 g; Diabetic Exchange: ½ lower fat meat

MISS DAISY'S SPINACH BALLS

1   10-ounce package frozen chopped spinach
½   cup very fine breadcrumbs
1   egg, lightly beaten
¼   cup part-skim ricotta cheese
¼   cup grated Parmesan cheese
3   green onions, chopped fine
¼   teaspoon ground cumin
2   teaspoons freshly squeezed lemon juice

Assemble all ingredients and utensils. Preheat the oven to 400°. Cook the spinach according to the package directions. Drain and squeeze out the excess water. Stir in the remaining ingredients and shape the mixture into 1-inch balls. Arrange the balls on a nonstick baking sheet. Bake at 400° for 12 to 15 minutes or until lightly browned. Yields 15 appetizers or 5 servings of 3 appetizers each.

Calories: 105; Fat: 4 g; Cholesterol: 62 mg; Sodium: 216 mg;
Carbohydrates: 11 g; Fiber: 1 g; Diabetic Exchange: ½ vegetable,
½ starch, ½ medium fat meat

CRAB AND CHEESE BALL

Great served on crackers or Melba toast, or with raw veggies.

4 *ounces crab meat, packed in water*
1 *8-ounce package Philadelphia Light Cream Cheese*
1 *teaspoon prepared horseradish*
1 *tablespoon lemon juice*
1 *teaspoon finely chopped onion*
1 *teaspoon finely chopped fresh chives*
¼ *teaspoon Worcestershire sauce*
   Paprika (optional)

Assemble all ingredients and utensils. Squeeze the excess water from the crab meat. In a mixing bowl combine all of the ingredients and blend well with a fork. Shape the mixture into a ball and sprinkle with paprika. Refrigerate for at least 1 hour. Yields 1½ cups or 22 servings of 1 tablespoon each.

Calories: 31; Fax: 2 g; Cholesterol: 12 mg; Sodium: 60 mg;
Carbohydrates: 0.4 g; Fiber: 0 g; Diabetic Exchange: ½ fat

CHERRY TOMATOES WITH PESTO FILLING

24   *cherry tomatoes*
1   *teaspoon dried leaf basil*
3   *tablespoons pine nuts, toasted*
1   *small clove garlic, minced*
1   *ounce Parmesan cheese*

Assemble all ingredients and utensils. Cut the tops off the tomatoes and hollow them out. Place the tomatoes on a baking sheet. In a food processor or blender combine the remaining ingredients and mix until the cheese and pine nuts are ground. Stuff the filling into the tomatoes and refrigerate until ready to serve. Serve cold or heat at 400° for 10 minutes. Yields 6 servings of 4 tomatoes each.

Calories: 72; Fat: 4 g; Cholesterol: 4 mg; Sodium: 97 mg;
Carbohydrates: 7 g; Fiber: 1 g; Diabetic Exchange: 1 vegetable, 1 fat

MUSHROOMS WITH DILLED TUNA

1   *3¼-ounce can water-packed tuna, drained*
¼   *teaspoon dried dillweed*
1   *tablespoon Dijon mustard*
1   *tablespoon fresh lime juice*
12   *capers, drained and chopped*
12   *medium mushrooms, stems removed*
    Fresh parsley sprigs
    Paprika

Assemble all ingredients and utensils. In a medium bowl combine the tuna, dillweed, mustard, lime juice, and capers. Stuff the mushrooms with the mixture. Garnish with fresh parsley sprigs and a sprinkle of paprika. Yields 12 servings.

Calories: 17; Fat: 0.1 g; Cholesterol: 2 mg; Sodium: 89 mg; Carbohydrates: 1 g; Fiber: 0 g; Diabetic Exchange: free (up to 3 mushrooms)

PECAN AND BEEF ROLL-UPS

Great as an appetizer, snack, or entrée.

4   ounces nonfat cream cheese, softened
2   tablespoons light cream cheese, softened
1   tablespoon nonfat mayonnaise
2   tablespoons finely chopped pecans
½   teaspoon dried dill
⅓   teaspoon garlic powder
1   2½-ounce package dried beef

Assemble all ingredients and utensils. In a large bowl beat together the cream cheeses and mayonnaise until soft. The mixture may be thinned with skim milk if it becomes too thick. Stir in the pecans and seasonings. Divide the spread evenly among the pieces of dried beef. Spread the mixture gently over each piece. Roll each piece of beef up, jelly-roll fashion. Refrigerate for 1 hour. Serve as a roll or slice into 1-inch slices. Yields 9 servings.

Calories: 44; Fat: 2 g; Cholesterol: 8 mg; Sodium: 374 mg; Carbohydrates: 1 g; Fiber: 0 g; Diabetic Exchange: ½ medium fat

BAKED PARMESAN CHICKEN STRIPS

Great as an appetizer or main course.

8	*4-ounce skinless, boneless chicken breast halves*
¼	*cup skim milk*
¼	*cup frozen egg substitute, thawed*
⅔	*cup fine dry breadcrumbs*
1	*cup grated Parmesan cheese*
1	*teaspoon dried leaf basil*
¾	*teaspoon dried leaf thyme*
½	*teaspoon onion powder*
¼	*teaspoon ground black pepper*

Assemble all ingredients and utensils. Preheat the oven to 400°. Spray a baking sheet with nonstick cooking spray. Cut the chicken into 4 x 1-inch strips. In a small bowl combine the milk and egg substitute, and set the mixture aside. In a separate bowl combine the breadcrumbs and remaining ingredients, mixing well. Dip the chicken into the milk mixture, then the breadcrumb mixture. Arrange the strips on the baking sheet. Bake at 400° for 15 to 18 minutes or until golden brown. Yields 54 chicken strips.

Calories: 32; Fat: 1 g; Cholesterol: 11 mg; Sodium: 51 mg;
Carbohydrates: 1 g; Fiber: 1 g; Diabetic Exchange: ½ lower fat meat

TURKEY PÂTÉ

Great with cherry tomatoes and gherkins.

1   *pound ground turkey*
1   *small clove garlic, minced*
1   *medium yellow onion, minced*
1   *teaspoon dried leaf basil*
½   *teaspoon ground thyme*
⅓   *teaspoon ground white pepper*
¼   *teaspoon salt*
1   *tablespoon apple juice*

Assemble all ingredients and utensils. In a nonstick skillet sauté the turkey, garlic, onion, basil, and thyme over medium heat until browned. Cool. Spoon the mixture into a food processor or blender. Add the remaining ingredients and process until smooth. Shape the pâté into a loaf. Cover and refrigerate for several hours or overnight. Yields 1½ cups or 6 servings of ¼ cup each.

Calories: 123; Fat: 7 g; Cholesterol: 67 mg; Sodium: 134 mg;
Carbohydrates: 2 g; Fiber: 0.1 g; Diabetic Exchange: 2 lower fat meat

HUMMUS

1   15-ounce can chick peas
2   tablespoons fresh lemon juice
⅓   cup sesame seeds, toasted
¼   cup chopped onion
2   cloves garlic, minced
2   teaspoons olive oil
2   teaspoons ground cumin
¼   teaspoon cayenne pepper

Assemble all ingredients and utensils. Drain the chick peas, reserving
½ cup of the liquid. Combine all the ingredients in a food processor or
blender. Process until smooth, adding the reserved liquid if needed to
thin the mixture. Transfer the mixture to a serving dish. Refrigerate for
several hours before serving to allow the flavors to blend. Yields 1½ cups
or 6 servings of ¼ cup each.

Calories: 192; Fat: 9 g; Cholesterol: 0 mg; Sodium: 231 mg;
Carbohydrates: 22 g; Fiber: 0.1 g; Diabetic Exchange: ½ medium fat meat,
1½ starch, 1 fat

SALSA

1   16-ounce can whole tomatoes
1   small green bell pepper, chopped
¼   cup chopped mild (yellow) onion
3   tablespoons chopped green onion
1   4-ounce can diced green chilies, rinsed and drained
3   tablespoons chopped fresh cilantro
½   clove garlic, minced

Assemble all ingredients and utensils. In a food processor or blender purée the tomatoes with their juice. Combine the remaining ingredients in a bowl and stir in the tomatoes. Cover and refrigerate. Will keep for up to a week in the refrigerator. Yields 2¼ cups or 9 servings of 4 tablespoons each.

Calories: 37; Fat: 1 g; Cholesterol: 0 mg; Sodium: 336 mg; Carbohydrates: 0.7 g; Fiber: 0.6 g; Diabetic Exchange: 1 vegetable

VEGGIE SALSA

Great served with chicken or tortilla chips.

1   14½-ounce can no-salt-added stewed tomatoes, undrained and chopped
1   8¾-ounce can no-salt-added whole kernel corn, drained
½   cup minced yellow onion
¼   cup minced fresh cilantro
1   tablespoon minced fresh chives
1   tablespoon apple cider vinegar
½   packet sugar substitute
1½ teaspoons safflower oil
1   jalapeño pepper, seeded and minced
1   clove garlic, minced

Assemble all ingredients and utensils. In a large bowl combine all of the ingredients and stir well. Cover and chill for at least 1 hour. Yields 3 cups or 54 servings of 1 tablespoon each.

Calories: 8; Fat: 0.2 g; Cholesterol: 0 mg; Sodium: 1 mg; Carbohydrates: 2 g; Fiber: 0.1 g; Diabetic Exchange: free (for 1 tablespoon)

MISS DAISY'S BLACK–EYED PEA SALSA

1   16-ounce package frozen black-eyed peas
¾   cup chopped green onions
½   cup diced red bell pepper
3   tablespoons apple cider vinegar
3   tablespoons oil-free Italian dressing
1   clove garlic, minced
¼   teaspoon hot sauce
¼   teaspoon salt
⅛   teaspoon ground black pepper

Assemble all ingredients and utensils. In a saucepan cook the peas according to the package directions. Do not add salt or fat. Drain. In a serving bowl combine the peas and the remaining ingredients. Cover and refrigerate for several hours before serving.

Variation: Add ½ cup of low-fat sour cream to the mixture to make a dip. The nutritional analysis is not based on sour cream being added. Yields 3½ cups or 56 servings of 1 tablespoon each.

Calories: 23; Fat: 0.2 g; Cholesterol: 0.1 mg; Sodium: 44 mg; Carbohydrates: 4 g; Fiber: 0.2 g; Diabetic Exchange: free

CHEESE TOASTIES

1   egg white, beaten
⅓   cup plain nonfat yogurt
½   teaspoon Worcestershire sauce
¼   teaspoon dry mustard
⅛   teaspoon cayenne pepper
½   cup grated farmer cheese
6   slices low-fat whole wheat bread
    Paprika

Assemble all ingredients and utensils. Preheat the oven to 350°. In a mixing bowl combine the egg white, yogurt, Worcestershire sauce, mustard, cayenne pepper, and farmer cheese, mixing well. Chill. Trim the crust from the bread. Spread 1 tablespoon of the cheese mixture on each slice. Cut each into 4 squares. Arrange the squares on a baking sheet. Sprinkle with paprika before baking. Bake at 350° for 10 minutes. Yields 24 servings of 1 square each.

Calories: 24; Fat: 1 g; Cholesterol: 1 mg; Sodium: 40 mg;
Carbohydrates: 3 g; Fiber: 0.4 g; Diabetic Exchange: free (for 1 square)

GUACAMOLE

Great with fajitas or as a chunky appetizer.

¼   cup finely chopped Roma tomatoes
1   tablespoon chopped green onion
½   small jalapeño pepper, seeded and finely chopped
1   clove garlic, minced
½   teaspoon lime juice
⅛   teaspoon salt
⅓   medium avocado, peeled and cut into small chunks

Assemble all ingredients and utensils. In a serving bowl combine all of the ingredients except the avocado and mix well. Toss the avocado in last and serve immediately. Yields ¾ cup or 6 servings of 2 tablespoons each.

Calories: 11; Fat: 1 g; Cholesterol: 0 mg; Sodium: 23 mg;
Carbohydrates: 1 g; Fiber: 0.5 g; Diabetic Exchange: free (for 2 tablespoons)

MISS DAISY'S PIMIENTO CHEESE

1   4-ounce can pimientos, drained and chopped
½   cup reduced-calorie mayonnaise
¼   cup Durkee's Sauce
2   tablespoons Dijon mustard
⅛   teaspoon cayenne pepper
1   clove garlic, minced
⅓   cup finely chopped fresh parsley
½   packet sugar substitute
1   pound (16 ounces) mild Cheddar cheese

Assemble all ingredients and utensils. In a large bowl combine all of the ingredients except the cheese. Mix well. Add the grated cheese and mix again. Refrigerate. Yields 3½ cups or 28 servings of 2 tablespoons each.

Calories: 89; Fat: 7 g; Cholesterol: 19 mg; Sodium: 166 mg;
Carbohydrates: 1 g; Fiber: 0 g; Diabetic Exchange: 1 meat, 1½ fat

7

BEVERAGES

ORANGE JULIUS

8 ounces nonfat plain yogurt
1 6-ounce can frozen orange juice concentrate
2½ cups skim milk
1 teaspoon vanilla extract

Assemble all ingredients and utensils. In a blender combine all of the ingredients and purée until smooth. Yields 6 servings of ¾ cup each.

Calories: 113; Fat: 0.5 g; Cholesterol: 3 mg; Sodium: 83 mg;
Carbohydrates: 21 g; Fiber: 0 g; Diabetic Exchange: ½ milk, 1 fruit

BANANA MILK SHAKE

½ medium banana
½ cup skim milk
⅓ teaspoon almond extract
½ packet sugar substitute

Assemble all ingredients and utensils. In a blender combine all of the ingredients and purée until smooth. Yields 1 serving of 8 ounces.

Calories: 90; Fat: 0.5 g; Cholesterol: 2 mg; Sodium: 65 mg;
Carbohydrates: 13 g; Fiber: 0 g; Diabetic Exchange: ½ milk, 1 fruit

CHOCOLATE MILK SHAKE

1   cup skim milk
2   teaspoons unsweetened cocoa
1   packet sugar substitute
3   to 4 ice cubes

Assemble all ingredients and utensils. In a blender or food processor combine all of the ingredients and purée on high speed until thickened.
Yields 1 serving of 8 ounces.

Calories: 99; Fat: 1 g; Cholesterol: 4 mg; Sodium: 126 mg;
Carbohydrates: 15 g; Fiber: 0 g; Diabetic Exchange: 1 milk

PINEAPPLE BANANA SHAKE

1   8-ounce can unsweetened crushed pineapple, undrained
1   cup skim milk
1   medium banana, cut into cubes
½   teaspoon vanilla extract
3   ice cubes

Assemble all ingredients and utensils. Drain the pineapple, reserving
¼ cup of juice. In a blender combine the pineapple, ¼ cup of juice, milk,
banana, vanilla, and ice cubes. Process until smooth. Serve immediately.
Yields 2 servings of 8 ounces each.

Calories: 170; Fat: 0.6 g; Cholesterol: 2 mg; Sodium: 65 mg;
Carbohydrates: 40 g; Fiber: 2 g; Diabetic Exchange: ½ milk, 2 fruit

STRAWBERRY SHAKE

1   cup skim milk
1   cup nonfat yogurt
1   tablespoon honey
2   teaspoons vanilla extract
2   cups unsweetened frozen strawberries, thawed

Assemble all ingredients and utensils. In a blender combine the skim milk, nonfat yogurt, honey, and vanilla. Gradually add the strawberries and blend until smooth. Yields 4 servings of 8 ounces each.

Calories: 96; Fat: 0.5 g; Cholesterol: 2 mg; Sodium: 78 mg; Carbohydrates: 19 g; Fiber: 0 g; Diabetic Exchanges: 1 milk

VANILLA MILK SHAKE

4   cups vanilla nonfat frozen yogurt
1¾ cups skim milk
½   teaspoon vanilla extract

Assemble all ingredients and utensils. In a blender or food processor combine all of the ingredients and blend until smooth and creamy. Yields 5 servings of 8 ounces each.

Calories: 192; Fat: 2 g; Cholesterol: 10 mg; Sodium: 133 mg; Carbohydrates: 33 g; Fiber: 0 g; Diabetic Exchange: 1 low-fat milk, 1 starch

BANANA SMOOTHIE

½   cup low-fat milk
¼   cup low-fat vanilla yogurt
½   medium banana
½   teaspoon vanilla extract
    Dash cinnamon

Assemble all ingredients and utensils. In a blender or food processor combine all of the ingredients and blend until smooth. Yields 1 serving of 8 ounces.

Calories: 163; Fat: 3 g; Cholesterol: 4 mg; Sodium: 106 mg;
Carbohydrates: 28 g; Fiber: 0.8 g; Diabetic Exchange: 1 fruit, 1 low-fat milk

PEACH SMOOTHIE

3   cups fresh peaches, peeled and sliced
2   cups low-fat plain yogurt
¼   cup honey
2   teaspoons fresh lemon juice
¼   teaspoon vanilla extract

Assemble all ingredients and utensils. In a blender combine all of the ingredients and blend until smooth. Pour into chilled glasses. Yields 4 servings of about ¾ cup each.

Calories: 192; Fat: 2 g; Cholesterol: 7 mg; Sodium: 81 mg;
Carbohydrates: 40 g; Fiber: 0 g; Diabetic Exchange: 1½ fruit, 1 low-fat milk

STRAWBERRY YOGURT SMOOTHIE

1   *cup fresh strawberries, sliced*
½   *cup low-fat yogurt*
½   *medium banana*
3   *ice cubes*
2   *whole fresh strawberries*

Assemble all ingredients and utensils. In a blender combine the sliced strawberries, yogurt, banana, and ice cubes. Process until smooth. Pour into 2 glasses and garnish each with a strawberry. Yields 2 servings of ¾ cup each.

Calories: 84; Fat: 1 g; Cholesterol: 3 mg; Sodium: 41 mg;
Carbohydrates: 16 g; Fiber: 2 g; Diabetic Exchange: ½ fruit, ½ milk

APPLE BERRY SPRITZER

1   *cup fresh strawberries*
½   *cup unsweetened apple juice*
½   *cup club soda*
    Fresh mint leaves

Assemble all ingredients and utensils. In a blender or food processor combine the strawberries and apple juice and puree until smooth. Stir in the club soda. Pour into glasses and garnish with fresh mint leaves. Yields 2 servings of ¾ cup each.

Calories: 52; Fat: 0.5 g; Cholesterol: 0 mg; Sodium: 15 mg;
Carbohydrates: 13 g; Fiber: 1 g; Diabetic Exchange: 1 fruit

BANANA RUM COCKTAIL

½   medium ripe banana
½   cup pineapple juice, unsweetened
¼   teaspoon rum extract

Assemble all ingredients and utensils. In a blender combine all of the ingredients and purée until smooth. Pour over ice. Yields 1 serving of 8 ounces.

Calories: 122; Fat: 0.3 g; Cholesterol: 0 mg; Sodium: 2 mg; Carbohydrates: 31 g; Fiber: 0.8 g; Diabetic Exchange: 2 fruit

CRANBERRY COOLER

¾   cup low-calorie cranberry juice
⅓   cup club soda
1   lime wedge

Assemble all ingredients and utensils. In a pitcher combine the cranberry juice and club soda. Pour over ice. Top with a lime wedge. Yields 1 serving of 8 ounces.

Calories: 34; Fat: 0 g; Cholesterol: 0 mg; Sodium: 22 mg; Carbohydrates: 8 g; Fiber: 0 g; Diabetic Exchange: ½ fruit

CRAN-ORANGE DRINK

1   *48-ounce bottle cranberry-apple juice cocktail*
1⅔ *cups unsweetened orange juice*
¼   *cup lemon juice*
3   *10- to 12-ounce bottles sparkling mineral water, chilled*

Assemble all ingredients and utensils. In a pitcher combine all of the ingredients. Serve cold. Yields 12 servings of 8 ounces each.

Calories: 98; Fat: 7 g; Cholesterol: 0 mg; Sodium: 4 mg;
Carbohydrates: 25 g; Fiber: 0 g; Diabetic Exchange:1½ fruit

RASPBERRY FIZZ

1   *16-ounce package frozen unsweetened raspberries, thawed*
1   *24-ounce bottle white grape juice, chilled*
1¾ *cups club soda, chilled*

Assemble all ingredients and utensils. In a blender purée the raspberries. Strain. In a pitcher combine the raspberry purée, grape juice, and club soda. Yields 6 servings of 8 ounces each.

Calories: 97; Fat: 0.5 g; Cholesterol: 0 mg; Sodium: 13 mg;
Carbohydrates: 24 g; Fiber: 2 g; Diabetic Exchange: 1½ fruit

MISS DAISY'S TEA PUNCH

10 *lemon-flavored tea bags*
2   *cups boiling water*
1¼ *cups fresh orange juice*
1   *6-ounce can frozen lemonade concentrate, thawed*
6   *packets sugar substitute*
8½ *cups cold water*

Assemble all ingredients and utensils. Place the tea bags in a pitcher or gallon jar, and add the water. Cover and steep for 5 minutes. Remove the tea bags and stir in the orange juice, lemonade concentrate, sugar substitute, and remaining cold water. Chill. Yields 12 servings of 8 ounces each.

Calories: 47; Fat: 0 g; Cholesterol: 0 mg; Sodium: 1 mg; Carbohydrates: 12 g; Fiber: 0 g; Diabetic Exchange: 1 fruit

LEMONADE

¼   *cup lemon juice*
¼   *cup apple juice concentrate*
2   *cups club soda*
18 *ice cubes*

Assemble all ingredients and utensils. In a blender combine all of the ingredients and blend well. Yields 4 servings of 8 ounces each.

Calories: 33; Fat: 0 g; Cholesterol: 0 mg; Sodium: 35 mg; Carbohydrates: 9 g; Fiber: 0 g; Diabetic Exchange: ½ fruit

SPICY TOMATO DRINK

5   *ounces low-sodium tomato juice*
⅛   *teaspoon ground oregano*
¼   *teaspoon pursley*
⅛   *teaspoon garlic powder*
½   *teaspoon Mrs. Dash or other salt substitute*
1   *teaspoon fresh lime juice*
⅛   *teaspoon ground black pepper*

Assemble all ingredients and utensils. In a blender combine all of the ingredients and blend well. Serve over ice cubes. Yields 1 serving of 8 ounces.

Calories: 29; Fat: 0.1 g; Cholesterol: 0 mg; Sodium: 15 mg;
Carbohydrates: 7 g; Fiber: 0 g; Diabetic Exchange: 1 vegetable

VEGGIE COCKTAIL

3   *cups no-salt-added tomato juice*
1   *slice yellow onion*
¼   *green bell pepper, chopped*
½   *cucumber, peeled and seeds removed*
2   *sprigs fresh parsley*
⅛   *teaspoon Tabasco sauce*
6   *lemon wedges or celery stalks*

Assemble all ingredients and utensils. In a blender combine all of the ingredients except the lemon wedges or celery stalks. Process until smooth. Chill.

Serve in glasses or mugs with a lemon wedge or celery stalk. Yields 6 servings of ¾ cup each.

Calories: 24; Fat: 0.1 g; Cholesterol: 0 mg; Sodium: 13 mg; Carbohydrates: 6 g; Fiber: 0.1 g; Diabetic Exchange: 1 vegetable

PARTY HOT SPICED TEA

12 cups water
1   teaspoon whole cloves
4   sticks cinnamon
6   regular tea bags
½   cup lemon juice
1½ cups unsweetened pineapple juice
1½ cups unsweetened orange juice
4   packets sugar substitute

Assemble all ingredients and utensils. In a saucepan combine the water, cloves, and cinnamon. Bring the mixture to a boil. Reduce the heat, cover, and simmer for 5 minutes. Remove the pan from the heat. Add the tea bags to the hot liquid and steep for 5 more minutes. Remove the tea bags and spices. Add the juices and sugar substitute, and serve. Yields 30 servings of 4 ounces each.

Calories: 14; Fat: 0 g; Cholesterol: 0 mg; Sodium: 2 mg;
Carbohydrates: 3 g; Fiber: 0 g; Diabetic Exchange: free

SPICED COCOA

2½   teaspoons unsweetened cocoa powder
½   teaspoon vanilla extract
6   ounces skim milk, heated
2   packets sugar substitute
1   tablespoon nondairy whipped topping
     Dash grated nutmeg

Assemble all ingredients and utensils. In a cup or glass combine the cocoa and vanilla. Add the warm milk and mix thoroughly. Stir in the sugar substitute. Add the whipped topping and nutmeg. Serve hot. Yields 1 serving of 8 ounces.

Calories: 92; Fat: 2 g; Cholesterol: 5 mg; Sodium: 99 mg; Carbohydrates: 13 g; Fiber: 0 g; Diabetic Exchange: 1 milk

HOT COCOA MIX

Place a cinnamon stick in each serving.
¾   cup unsweetened cocoa
¼   teaspoon salt
1   quart instant nonfat dry milk
     Sugar substitute equivalent to 1½ cups sugar

Assemble all ingredients and utensils. In a mixing bowl combine all of the ingredients and mix well. Store in an airtight container in a cool place.

To serve, use 2 tablespoons of mix per 6 ounces of boiling water. Serve with a stick of cinnamon. Yields 32 servings of 6 ounces.

Calories: 36; Fat: 0.2 g; Cholesterol: 2 mg; Sodium: 63 mg; Carbohydrates: 6 g; Fiber: 0 g; Diabetic Exchange: ½ milk

~ 8 ~

SOUPS

MISS DAISY'S GAZPACHO

2   cups peeled, coarsely chopped tomatoes
1½ cups no-salt-added tomato juice
¾   cup peeled, seeded, and diced cucumber
3   tablespoons chopped fresh parsley
2   tablespoons chopped green onions
1   tablespoon balsamic vinegar
1   small clove garlic, minced
½   teaspoon ground cumin
⅛   teaspoon cayenne (hot) pepper
⅛   teaspoon salt
⅛   teaspoon freshly ground black pepper

Assemble all ingredients and utensils. Purée all ingredients in a blender or food processor. Chill for at least 2 hours. Serve cold. Yields 4 servings of 8 ounces each.

Calories: 40; Fat: 0.4 g; Cholesterol: 0 mg; Sodium: 86 mg; Carbohydrates: 9 g; Fiber: 0.8 g; Diabetic Exchange: 1 vegetable

TOMATO BASIL SOUP

8   cups peeled, seeded, and diced tomatoes
1   cup chopped celery
1   cup chopped onion
2   cups water
2   teaspoons chicken-flavored bouillon granules
½   teaspoon freshly ground black pepper
⅔   cup chopped fresh basil
1   packet sugar substitute, optional

Assemble all ingredients and utensils. Spray a large soup pot or Dutch oven with vegetable cooking spray. Over medium heat sauté the tomatoes, celery, and onion for 5 minutes or until the onion is tender. Add the water, chicken granules, and pepper and bring the mixture to a boil. Cover, reduce the heat, and simmer for 30 minutes, stirring occasionally. Transfer the mixture in batches to a food processor or blender and purée until smooth. To serve cold stir in chopped basil and sugar substitute, and chill. To serve hot: Return to soup pot and stir in basil and sugar substitute. Reheat. Yields 8 servings of 8 ounces each.

Calories: 49; Fat: 0.5 g; Cholesterol: 0 mg; Sodium: 33 mg;
Carbohydrates: 11 g; Fiber: 2 g; Diabetic Exchange: 2 vegetable

COLD TOMATO/SHRIMP SOUP

1   cup tomato juice
½   cup cooked fresh or frozen shrimp
2   tablespoons lemon juice
½   teaspoon prepared horseradish
¼   teaspoon Worcestershire sauce
⅛   teaspoon Tabasco sauce

Assemble all ingredients and utensils. In a large serving bowl, combine all of the ingredients. Chill before serving. Yields 1¼ cups or 1 serving.

Calories: 106; Fat: 1 g; Cholesterol: 111 mg; Sodium: 675 mg; Carbohydrates: 13 g; Fiber: 0 g; Diabetic Exchange: 1 lower fat meat, 2 vegetables

VICHYSSOISE (POTATO SOUP)

1   cup canned no-salt-added chicken broth, undiluted
1   medium-size potato, peeled and diced
2   leeks, well washed, sliced
2   cups skim milk
¼   teaspoon salt
¼   teaspoon ground white pepper
1   tablespoon part-skim ricotta cheese
1   tablespoon chopped fresh chives

Assemble all ingredients and utensils. In a large saucepan or soup pot combine the chicken broth, potato, and leeks. Bring the broth to a boil and cook until the potato is tender, about 15 minutes. Place the potato mixture in a food processor or blender and add the milk, salt, pepper, and ricotta. Purée until smooth. Chill before serving. Garnish with chives. Yields 4 cups or 4 servings of 8 ounces each.

Calories: 124; Fat: 1 g; Cholesterol: 3 mg; Sodium: 218 mg; Carbohydrates: 23 g; Fiber: 1 g; Diabetic Exchange: 1 skim milk

CHILLED MELON SOUP

2   *cups chopped cantaloupe*
2   *cups chopped honeydew melon*
1   *cup fresh orange juice*
2   *tablespoons lime juice*

Assemble all ingredients and utensils. In a blender combine all of the ingredients. Purée until smooth. Chill before serving. Yields 6 servings of 6 ounces each.

Calories: 59; Fat: 0.3 g; Cholesterol: 0 mg; Sodium: 11 mg; Carbohydrates: 14 g; Fiber: 0.4 g; Diabetic Exchange: 1 fruit

CREAM OF ASPARAGUS SOUP

1   *cup water*
2   *cups fresh asparagus, washed, trimmed, and sliced*
2   *tablespoons cornstarch*
2   *tablespoons water*
1   *tablespoon reduced-calorie margarine*
2   *cups skim milk*
¼   *teaspoon ground white pepper*

Assemble all ingredients and utensils. In a large saucepan bring 1 cup of water to a boil. Add the asparagus. Reduce the heat, cover, and simmer for 10 minutes or until the asparagus is tender. Drain.

Mix the cornstarch and 2 tablespoons of water to make a smooth paste. In a small saucepan melt the margarine over medium heat. Add the cornstarch mixture, stirring constantly to prevent lumping. Continue stirring while adding the milk. Cook over low heat, stirring occasionally, until the mixture begins to thicken. Remove the pan from the heat and allow the mixture to cool. Combine the milk mixture and asparagus in a blender or food processor and process until smooth. Season with pepper.

Serve hot in bowls, over toast points if desired. Yields 8 servings of 4 ounces each.

Calories: 46; Fat: 1 g; Cholesterol: 1 mg; Sodium: 50 mg;
Carbohydrates: 6 g; Fiber: 0.3 g; Diabetic Exchange: ½ starch

CHILI CON CARNE

1   *pound extra lean ground beef*
1   *pound ground turkey, lowest fat*
2   *tablespoons chili powder*
¼   *teaspoon cayenne pepper*
¼   *teaspoon paprika*
3   *15-ounce cans kidney beans, drained*
2   *large yellow onions, chopped*
2   *green bell peppers, chopped*
2   *16-ounce cans diced tomatoes with juice*
2   *8-ounce cans tomato sauce*
2   *bay leaves, whole*

Assemble all ingredients and utensils. Spray a large stock pot with cooking spray. Brown the beef and turkey. Add the remaining ingredients and simmer for 1 hour and 30 minutes. Remove the bay leaf before serving. Yields 12 servings of 8 ounces each.

Calories: 259; Fat: 8 g; Cholesterol: 56 mg; Sodium: 865 mg;
Carbohydrates: 28 g; Fiber: 2 g; Diabetic Exchange: 2 meat, 2 vegetable, 1 starch

LEEK SOUP

1½ cups minced fresh leeks with some greens
1   clove garlic, minced
1   cup chopped yellow onion
1   quart low-fat or defatted chicken stock
2   cups diced raw red potatoes
1   cup skim evaporated milk
⅓   teaspoon ground white pepper

Assemble all ingredients and utensils. In a stock pot, cook the leeks, garlic, and onion in 1 cup of stock for 5 minutes. Add the remaining stock and the potatoes. Bring to a boil, reduce the heat and simmer 25 minutes. Add the milk. Remove the pan from the heat and allow the mixture to cool. Whip with a whisk or purée in a blender until smooth. Serve hot. Season with pepper. Yields 10 servings of 4 ounces each.

Calories: 64; Fat: 0.2 g; Cholesterol: 1 mg; Sodium: 37 mg; Carbohydrates: 13 g; Fiber: 0.5 g; Diabetic Exchange: 1 starch

FRENCH ONION SOUP

1½ cups thinly sliced yellow onions
6   cups salt-free beef broth
¼   teaspoon ground black pepper
6   slices French bread, toasted
3   ounces grated low-fat mozzarella cheese

Assemble all ingredients and utensils. In a large pot combine the onions, beef broth, and black pepper. Simmer over low heat for 30 minutes. When ready to serve, divide the soup into 6 ovenproof bowls. Top each with a slice of toasted French bread and ½ ounce of cheese. Broil until the cheese is melted. Yields 6 servings of 6 ounces each.

Calories: 163; Fat: 3 g; Cholesterol: 9 mg; Sodium: 279 mg; Carbohydrates: 25 g; Fiber: 0.3 g; Diabetic Exchange: ½ starch, ½ medium fat

WHITE BEAN AND BARLEY SOUP

¼   *cup water*
½   *cup chopped yellow onion*
1   *cup grated carrots*
1   *cup peeled and sliced Idaho potatoes*
6   *cups low-fat chicken broth*
1   *clove garlic, minced*
½   *teaspoon ground black pepper*
1   *cup cooked white beans*
¼   *cup barley*

Assemble all ingredients and utensils. In a large saucepan sauté the onion in water until clear. Add the next 5 ingredients. Bring to a boil and then reduce the heat. Simmer about 15 to 20 minutes, until the vegetables are tender. Add the cooked beans and barley, and cook for another 30 minutes. Stir occasionally, adding more stock if necessary. Yields 4 servings of 8 ounces each.

Calories: 174; Fat: 0.5 g; Cholesterol: 0 mg; Sodium: 23 mg; Carbohydrates: 35 g; Fiber: 2 g; Diabetic Exchange: 2 starch, 1 vegetable

WHITE BEAN SOUP

3   to 4 cloves garlic, crushed
1   cup chopped onion
1   tablespoon olive oil
1   carrot, sliced
1   stalk celery, chopped
4   cups water
2   cups (16 ounces) cooked white beans
¼   cup sliced black olives
1   tablespoon freshly squeezed lemon juice
2   teaspoons fresh chopped tarragon
⅛   teaspoon salt
⅛   teaspoon freshly ground black pepper

Assemble all ingredients and utensils. In a large soup pot or Dutch oven sauté the garlic and onion in oil. Stir in the carrot and celery. Add the remaining ingredients and simmer for 45 minutes. Serve hot. Yields 6 servings of 8 ounces each.

Calories: 131; Fat: 4 g; Cholesterol: 0 mg; Sodium: 109 mg; Carbohydrates: 20 g; Fiber: 1 g; Diabetic Exchange: 1 starch, 1 vegetable, 1 fat

BLACK BEAN SOUP

30 ounces canned black beans
2   cups low-fat chicken broth
2   cups water
1   carrot, sliced
1   large yellow onion, chopped
1   medium Idaho potato, grated
2   stalks celery, chopped
1   teaspoon dried leaf oregano
1   teaspoon cumin
⅛   teaspoon cayenne pepper
2   tablespoons fresh chopped cilantro
⅓   cup lemon juice
    Plain nonfat yogurt for garnish
    Paprika for garnish

Assemble all ingredients and utensils. In a large stock pot combine the beans, broth, water, carrot, onion, potato, celery, oregano, cumin, cayenne, and cilantro. Cook over medium heat for 20 minutes. Stir in the lemon juice just before serving. Garnish each serving with 1 tablespoon of yogurt and ⅛ teaspoon of paprika. Yields 6 servings of 8 ounces each.

Calories: 226; Fat: 1 g; Cholesterol: 0 mg; Sodium: 354 mg;
Carbohydrates: 42 g; Fiber: 2 g; Diabetic Exchange: 2½ starch,
1 vegetable, 1 lower fat meat

TWO BEANS AND A PEA

1   28-ounce can unsalted diced tomatoes
1   cup water
1   6-ounce can tomato paste
1½ teaspoons chopped garlic
1   teaspoon chili powder
1   tablespoon Dijon mustard
1   teaspoon dried leaf basil
1   teaspoon dried leaf oregano
½   teaspoon ground cumin
½   teaspoon ground black pepper
1   15-ounce can kidney beans, drained
1   15-ounce can garbanzo beans, drained
1   15-ounce can black-eyed peas, drained
1   cup chopped celery
1   cup sliced carrots
1   medium yellow onion, chopped

Assemble all ingredients and utensils. In a large pot combine all of the
ingredients except the celery, carrots, and onion and bring the mixture to
a boil. Reduce the heat, cover, and simmer for 10 minutes. Stir in the
fresh vegetables and simmer, covered, for an additional 20 to 25 minutes.
Yields 12 servings of 8 ounces each.

Calories: 155; Fat: 2 g; Cholesterol: 0 mg; Sodium: 523 mg;
Carbohydrates: 30 g; Fiber: 0.8 g; Diabetic Exchange: 1 vegetable, 1½ starch

SPLIT PEA SOUP

1   cup green or yellow split peas, soaked overnight
6   cups water
1   tablespoon low-sodium chicken or vegetable bouillon granules
1   carrot, sliced
1   medium yellow onion, chopped
⅛   teaspoon dried leaf marjoram
⅛   teaspoon dried leaf thyme
⅛   teaspoon ground red pepper
1   teaspoon imitation bacon bits

Assemble all ingredients and utensils. Drain the split peas. In a large soup pot or Dutch oven combine all of the ingredients except the bacon bits. Bring the mixture to a boil. Cover, reduce the heat, and simmer for 45 minutes, until tender. Serve warm. Sprinkle ¼ teaspoon of bacon bits over each serving. Yields 4 servings of 8 ounces each.

Calories: 167; Fat: 1 g; Cholesterol: 0 mg; Sodium: 481 mg;
Carbohydrates: 30 g; Fiber: 3 g; Diabetic Exchange: 2 starch, 1 bread, 1 vegetable

LIMA BEAN SOUP

2   *cups dried lima beans, washed and drained*
½   *cup finely chopped yellow onion*
1   *carrot, peeled and thinly sliced*
2   *cloves garlic, chopped*
1   *stalk celery, chopped*
1   *8-ounce can tomatoes, crushed*
½   *cup chopped fresh parsley*
1   *teaspoon low-sodium soy sauce*
8   *cups water*

Assemble all ingredients and utensils. In a large soup pot or Dutch oven combine all of the ingredients. Bring the mixture to a boil. Reduce the heat and simmer for 1 hour and 30 minutes to 2 hours, or until the beans are tender. Add additional water if necessary to keep the mixture from becoming too thick. Yields 8 servings of 8 ounces each.

Calories: 143; Fat: 0.5 g; Cholesterol: 0 mg; Sodium: 109 mg;
Carbohydrates: 28 g; Fiber: 5 g; Diabetic Exchange: 1½ starch, 1 vegetable

VEGETABLE SOUP

2   13¾-ounce cans no-salt-added beef broth
1¾ cups peeled, diced potato
2   cups chopped onion
1   cup chopped celery
1   cup sliced carrots
½   cup water
1   teaspoon dried leaf basil
½   teaspoon freshly ground pepper
¼   teaspoon salt
¼   teaspoon dried thyme
2   bay leaves
3   14½-ounce cans no-salt-added whole tomatoes, undrained
1   10-ounce package frozen whole kernel corn
1   10-ounce package frozen cut okra
1   10-ounce package frozen baby lima beans

Assemble all ingredients and utensils. In a large soup pot or Dutch oven combine all of the ingredients except the corn, okra, and lima beans. Bring to a boil. Reduce the heat, cover, and simmer for 45 minutes.

Add the corn, okra, and lima beans. Return the soup to a boil, reduce the heat, and simmer for another 20 to 30 minutes. Discard the bay leaves and serve warm. Yields 16 servings of 8 ounces each.

Calories: 84; Fat: 0.6 g; Cholesterol: 0 mg; Sodium: 151 mg; Carbohydrates: 18 g; Fiber: 2 g; Diabetic Exchange: 1 starch

CREAMY VEGETABLE SOUP

2   *cups low-fat chicken broth*
1   *cup sliced carrots*
1   *cup sliced yellow squash*
½   *cup sliced turnips*
2   *tablespoons chopped onion*
¼   *teaspoon white pepper*
¼   *teaspoon celery seed*
½   *cup skim milk*

Assemble all ingredients and utensils. In a large saucepan bring the broth to a boil and add the vegetables and seasonings. Reduce the heat and simmer for 15 to 20 minutes or until the vegetables are cooked. Add the skim milk and keep warm until ready to serve. Yields 6 servings of ¾ cup each.

Calories: 26; Fat: 0.2 g; Cholesterol: trace; Sodium: 79 mg;
Carbohydrates: 5 g; Fiber: 0.6 g; Diabetic Exchange: 1 vegetable

NEW ENGLAND CLAM CHOWDER

6   tablespoons margarine
2   cups chopped celery
2   cloves garlic, minced
2   cups chopped yellow onions
¼   cup all-purpose flour
2   cups skim milk
1   cup peeled and diced potatoes
1   pound fresh or frozen shucked clams
1   tablespoon dried leaf thyme
½   teaspoon salt

Assemble all ingredients and utensils. In a skillet melt 2 tablespoons of margarine. Add the celery, garlic, and onions, and sauté over medium heat for 5 minutes, until the celery is tender. Melt the remaining margarine in a large saucepan and stir in the flour. Cook over medium heat for 3 to 5 minutes, until the mixture starts to brown, stirring constantly. Gradually add the skim milk, stirring rapidly to prevent lumps from forming. Add the potatoes and cook for 10 minutes, stirring occasionally. Add the sautéed vegetables, clams, thyme, and salt. Simmer until the potatoes are tender. Yields 8 servings of 4 ounces each.

Calories: 192; Fat: 0.5 g; Cholesterol: 6 mg; Sodium: 347 mg; Carbohydrates: 15 g; Fiber: 1 g; Diabetic Exchange: ½ milk, 2 lower fat meat, 1 starch, 3 fat, 1 vegetable

CHICKEN NOODLE SOUP

4   6-ounce skinless, boneless chicken breasts
2   cups water
1   teaspoon celery seed
¾   teaspoon poultry seasoning
¼   teaspoon dried leaf thyme
1   cup water
3   ounces medium egg noodles, uncooked
½   cup diced celery
½   cup diced carrot
¼   cup sliced green onions
1   teaspoon chicken-flavored bouillon granules
1   bay leaf

Assemble all ingredients and utensils. In a large soup pot or Dutch oven combine the chicken, 2 cups of water, celery seed, poultry seasoning, and thyme and bring the mixture to a boil. Reduce the heat, cover, and simmer for 45 minutes or until the chicken is tender.

Remove the chicken from the broth, reserving the broth. Let the chicken cool. Coarsely chop the chicken and set it aside. Skim the fat from the broth and strain the broth through a double layer of cheesecloth, discarding the herbs.

Clean the soup pot and return the broth to it. Add 1 cup of water and the remaining ingredients. Bring the soup to a boil. Reduce the heat, cover, and simmer for 20 minutes, stirring frequently. Add the chopped chicken and return the soup to a boil. Reduce the heat and simmer for 5 minutes. Remove the bay leaf before serving. Serve hot. Yields 1½ quarts or 6 servings of 8 ounces each.

Calories: 191; Fat: 2 g; Cholesterol: 81 mg; Sodium: 95 mg; Carbohydrates: 12 g; Fiber: 0.2 g; Diabetic Exchange: 4 lower fat meat, 1 starch

CORN CHOWDER

1   *teaspoon olive oil*
1   *cup diced red bell pepper*
1   *cup chopped onion*
2   *tablespoons all-purpose flour*
½   *teaspoon ground cumin*
⅛   *teaspoon ground red pepper*
2   *cups water*
1½ *cups peeled, diced potato*
1   *teaspoon chicken-flavored bouillon granules*
2   *cups frozen whole kernel corn*
2   *tablespoons canned chopped green chilies, drained*
½   *teaspoon freshly ground black pepper*
1   *cup evaporated skim milk*

Assemble all ingredients and utensils. In a large soup pot or Dutch oven heat the olive oil and sauce the red pepper and onion until tender, about 5 minutes.

Stir in the flour, cumin, and ground red pepper. Cook for 1 minute, stirring constantly. Gradually stir in the water. Add the potato and bouillon granules. Bring the mixture to a boil, stirring constantly. Reduce the heat, cover, and simmer for about 15 minutes, until the potato is tender and the mixture is thickened. Add the corn and remaining ingredients. Cook until thoroughly heated. Yields 1½ quarts or 6 servings of 8 ounces each.

Calories: 145; Fat: 2 g; Cholesterol: 2 mg; Sodium: 89 mg; Carbohydrates: 29 g; Fiber: 2 g; Diabetic Exchange: 2 starch

MISS DAISY'S BROCCOLI CHEESE SOUP

6   cups fresh broccoli flowerets
1   quart water
1   cup chopped onion
1   clove garlic, minced
1   cup plain nonfat yogurt
⅓   cup all-purpose flour
2   10½-ounce cans low-sodium chicken broth
1   cup water
¼   teaspoon salt
¼   teaspoon ground black pepper
1   cup shredded reduced-fat sharp Cheddar cheese

Assemble all ingredients and utensils. In a large soup pot or Dutch oven bring the water to a boil. Add the broccoli and cook for 5 to 7 minutes or until tender. Drain well and set aside.

Spray a large skillet with vegetable spray and sauté the onion and garlic over medium heat until tender. Drain.

In a large saucepan combine the yogurt and flour; stirring well with a wire whisk. Add the broth, water, salt, and pepper. Cook over medium heat for 30 minutes or until thickened and bubbly, stirring often. Add the broccoli and onion mixtures and the shredded cheese, stirring until the cheese melts. Serve warm. Sprinkle with paprika, if desired. Yields 8 servings of 8 ounces each.

Calories: 105; Fat: 3 g; Cholesterol: 11 mg; Sodium: 223 mg;
Carbohydrates: 12 g; Fiber: 1 g; Diabetic Exchange: 1 low-fat milk, 1 vegetable

9

SALADS

CRANBERRY RELISH

1   medium orange, peeled, sectioned, and seeded
1   medium lemon, peeled, sectioned, and seeded
2   cups fresh cranberries, rinsed
1   8-ounce can unsweetened chunk pineapple, drained
½   cup maple syrup

Assemble all ingredients and utensils. In a food processor or blender combine the orange sections, lemon sections, cranberries, pineapple, and maple syrup. Pulse until finely chopped. Transfer the mixture to a saucepan and simmer over low to medium heat for 5 minutes or until it just starts to thicken. Cool and serve. The relish will keep for several weeks in the refrigerator. *Note:* This relish is also delicious served raw. Yields 1½ cups or 6 servings of ¼ cup each.

Calories: 108; Fat: 0.2 g; Cholesterol: 0 mg; Sodium: 4 mg; Carbohydrates: 28 g; Fiber: 1 g; Diabetic Exchange: 1 fruit, 1 starch

MISS DAISY'S FESTIVE CRANBERRY SALAD

1   *envelope sugar-free unflavored gelatin*
½   *cup cold water*
1   *teaspoon grated orange rind*
1   *16-ounce can whole berry cranberry sauce*
1   *8-ounce can crushed pineapple, undrained*
½   *cup finely chopped apple*
¼   *cup diced celery*

Assemble all ingredients and utensils. In a saucepan combine the gelatin and cold water; let the gelatin soften for 1 minute. Cook over low heat, stirring constantly, until the gelatin dissolves.

Remove the pan from the heat and stir in the orange rind. Chill for 30 to 45 minutes. Mix in the cranberry sauce, pineapple, apple, and celery. Pour the mixture into a 1½-quart casserole or mold. Cover and chill until firm. Yields 8 servings of ¾ cup each.

Calories: 105; Fat: 0.1 g; Cholesterol: 0 mg; Sodium: 15 mg; Carbohydrates: 27 g; Fiber: 0.4 g; Diabetic Exchange: 2 fruit

CARROT RAISIN SALAD

2   *cups coarsely shredded carrots*
¼   *cup raisins*
1   *8-ounce can crushed pineapple in juice, drained*
¼   *cup vanilla low-fat yogurt*
2   *tablespoons nonfat mayonnaise*
1   *teaspoon reduced-fat creamy peanut butter*
¼   *teaspoon ground cinnamon*

Assemble all ingredients and utensils. In a medium bowl combine the carrots, raisins, and pineapple, and mix well. In a separate bowl combine the yogurt and remaining ingredients. Add the carrot mixture. Mix well. Cover and chill thoroughly. Yields 6 servings of ½ cup each.

Calories: 76; Fat: 0.7 g; Cholesterol: 0.6 mg; Sodium: 56 mg; Carbohydrates: 17 g; Fiber: 1 g; Diabetic Exchange: 1 fruit, ½ vegetable

ORANGE SPINACH SALAD

3   large oranges, peeled and sectioned
½   pound fresh spinach, washed and stems removed
1   6-ounce can sliced water chestnuts, drained
¼   cup thinly sliced red onions
¼   cup plain nonfat yogurt
3   tablespoons nonfat mayonnaise
1   tablespoon honey
1   tablespoon skim milk
1   teaspoon poppy seeds

Assemble all ingredients and utensils. In a large bowl combine the oranges, spinach, water chestnuts, and red onions. Toss gently. In a separate bowl combine the remaining ingredients. Pour 1 tablespoon of the poppy seed dressing over each serving. Yields 8 servings of ½ cup with 1 tablespoon of dressing each.

Calories: 61; Fat: 0.4 g; Cholesterol: 0.2 mg; Sodium: 69 mg; Carbohydrates: 14 g; Fiber: 1 g; Diabetic Exchange: ½ fruit, 1 vegetable

CONGEALED ORANGE CARROT SALAD

2 *envelopes unflavored gelatin*
½ *cup cold water*
1 *cup unsweetened pineapple juice*
1 *tablespoon honey*
½ *cup fresh orange juice*
1 *cup grated carrots*
1 *cup orange segments, cut in small pieces*
1½ *cups unsweetened crushed pineapple, drained*
   Green leaf lettuce for garnish
½ *cup nonfat yogurt for garnish*

Assemble all ingredients and utensils. In a small bowl soften the gelatin in cold water. In a saucepan heat the pineapple juice. Remove the pan from the heat and stir in the softened gelatin. Stir to dissolve. Add the honey and orange juice. Refrigerate until the mixture begins to thicken. Fold in the carrots, oranges, and pineapple. Pour the mixture into a 1½-quart casserole or mold and refrigerate. Garnish with lettuce and yogurt. Yields 4 cups or 8 servings of ½ cup each.

Calories: 90; Fat: 0.2 g; Cholesterol: 0.3 mg; Sodium: 17 mg; Carbohydrates: 20 g; Fiber: 0.7 g; Diabetic Exchange: 1 fruit, ½ starch

STRAWBERRY SPINACH SALAD

10 *ounces spinach, washed and stems removed*
1 *cup strawberries, hulled and halved*
¼ *cup thinly sliced mushrooms*
½ *cup Poppy Seed Dressing (see recipe, p. 135)*

Assemble all ingredients and utensils. Divide the spinach evenly among 4 serving plates. Place the strawberries and mushrooms on the spinach.

Pour 2 tablespoons of dressing over each salad. Yields 4 servings of ½ cup each.

Calories: 42; Fat: 0.5 g; Cholesterol: 0.3 mg; Sodium: 67 mg;
Carbohydrates: 8 g; Fiber: 3 g; Diabetic Exchange: ½ starch

SIX CUP FRUIT SALAD

1   cup unsweetened sliced peaches, drained
1   cup unsweetened pineapple chunks, drained
1   cup unsweetened sliced pears, drained
1   cup unsweetened sliced apricots, drained
1   cup fruit-flavored nonfat yogurt
1   cup Homemade Whipped Topping (see recipe, p. 253)

Assemble all ingredients and utensils. In a large serving bowl combine all of the ingredients. Refrigerate until chilled. Yields 10 servings of ½ cup each.

Calories: 67; Fat: 0.1 g; Cholesterol: 0.7 mg; Sodium: 25 mg;
Carbohydrates: 16 g; Fiber: 0.5 g; Diabetic Exchange: 1 fruit

GREEK SALAD

1   green bell pepper, sliced
1   red bell pepper, sliced
1   yellow bell pepper, sliced
1   unpeeled cucumber, sliced
3   tablespoons lemon juice
3   tablespoons red wine vinegar
¼   cup pitted whole black olives, chopped
¼   teaspoon dried leaf oregano
4   ounces feta cheese, crumbled

Assemble all ingredients and utensils. In a medium bowl mix together the peppers and cucumber. Add the lemon juice, vinegar, olives, and oregano. Stir until mixed. Cover and marinate for several hours. Toss well and stir in the crumbled feta cheese before serving. Yields 8 servings of 1 cup each.

Calories: 60; Fat: 4 g; Cholesterol: 13 mg; Sodium: 197 mg; Carbohydrates: 4 g; Fiber: 0.5 g; Diabetic Exchange: 1 vegetable, 1 fat

SOUTHERN POTATO SALAD

4	large red, new potatoes, washed
¼	cup plain nonfat yogurt
2	tablespoons reduced-calorie mayonnaise
1	tablespoon Dijon mustard
1	cup chopped celery
1	small red onion, chopped
¼	cup pickle relish, drained
¼	teaspoon salt
¼	teaspoon ground black pepper
2	teaspoons celery seeds

Assemble all ingredients and utensils. Boil the potatoes until tender, about 15 to 20 minutes. Drain. Chill the potatoes and then dice them. In a large bowl combine the remaining ingredients. Add the diced potatoes and sprinkle with celery seeds. Yields 4 cups or 6 servings of ¾ cup each.

Calories: 129; Fat: 2 g; Cholesterol: 2 mg; Sodium: 294 mg; Carbohydrates: 25 g; Fiber: 0.6 g; Diabetic Exchange: 1 starch, 1 vegetable, ½ fat

THREE-BEAN SALAD

1   *cup cooked pinto beans, drained*
1   *cup cooked white beans, drained*
1   *cup chopped cooked fresh green beans, drained*
½   *cup thinly sliced red onion*
2   *green onions, sliced*
2   *tablespoons minced fresh parsley*
1   *small clove garlic, minced*
¼   *cup red wine vinegar*
2   *teaspoons frozen apple juice concentrate*
¼   *teaspoon freshly ground black pepper*

Assemble all ingredients and utensils. In a large bowl combine the pinto beans, white beans, green beans, red onion, green onions, and parsley. In a separate bowl whisk together the remaining ingredients. Pour the mixture over the beans. Toss. Yields 4 cups or 6 servings of ¾ cup each.

Calories: 99; Fat: 0.4 g; Cholesterol: 0 mg; Sodium: 5 mg;
Carbohydrates: 19 g; Fiber: 2 g; Diabetic Exchange: 1 starch, ½ vegetable

MISS DAISY'S BLACK BEAN SALAD

3   cups cooked black beans
1   red bell pepper, chopped
½   green bell pepper, chopped
⅓   medium red onion, chopped
2   green onions, sliced
1   rib celery, finely chopped
3   Italian plum tomatoes, seeded and chopped
1   cup cooked white rice
1   teaspoon olive oil
1   tablespoon orange juice
1   tablespoon lemon juice
¼   teaspoon hot pepper sauce
½   teaspoon ground cumin
¼   teaspoon salt

Assemble all ingredients and utensils. In a large bowl carefully combine the first 8 ingredients. In a separate bowl whisk together the remaining ingredients. Pour the dressing over the salad and toss. Yields 6 cups or 8 servings of ¾ cup each.

Calories: 121; Fat: 1 g; Cholesterol: 0 mg; Sodium: 91 mg; Carbohydrates: 22 g; Fiber: 3 g; Diabetic Exchange: 1½ starch

SEVEN LAYER VEGETABLE SALAD

2   cups halved cherry tomatoes
1½ cups fresh spinach torn into bite-size pieces
1½ cups cauliflower flowerets
½   small head red cabbage, thinly sliced
¾   cups sliced fresh mushrooms
2   medium zucchini, sliced
½   cup reduced-calorie mayonnaise
¼   cup buttermilk
1   clove garlic, minced
¼   cup crumbled blue cheese
¼   cup minced chives

Assemble all ingredients and utensils. In a 2-quart casserole dish arrange the tomatoes cut side down. Layer the spinach, cauliflower, cabbage, mushrooms, and zucchini over the tomatoes. Mix the mayonnaise, buttermilk, and garlic. Spread the mayonnaise mixture over the top of the salad. Sprinkle blue cheese and chives over all. Cover and refrigerate for several hours or overnight. Toss before serving. Yields 8 servings of ¾ cup each.

Calories: 96; Fat: 7 g; Cholesterol: 8 g; Sodium: 200 mg;
Carbohydrates: 7 g; Fiber: 1 g; Diabetic Exchange: 1 vegetable, 1 fat

MARINATED COLESLAW

3   cups coarsely shredded cabbage
1½   cups coarsely shredded carrots
½   cup sliced green onions
½   cup apple cider vinegar
½   cup unsweetened apple juice
¾   tablespoon prepared mustard
½   teaspoon ground black pepper
⅛   teaspoon garlic powder
¼   teaspoon salt

Assemble all ingredients and utensils. In a large bowl combine the cabbage, carrot, and green onions. In a separate bowl mix together the vinegar and remaining ingredients. Pour the dressing mixture over the cabbage mixture, tossing well. Cover and refrigerate overnight. Yields 6 servings of ½ cup each.

Calories: 38; Fat: 0.2 g; Cholesterol: 0 mg; Sodium: 130 mg; Carbohydrates: 9 g; Fiber: 0.8 g; Diabetic Exchange: 1 vegetable

FAVORITE COLESLAW

1½ teaspoons prepared mustard
    Sugar substitute equal to ¼ cup sugar
1   tablespoon vegetable oil
¼   teaspoon salt
¼   teaspoon celery seed
2   tablespoons white vinegar
3   cups shredded cabbage
1½ cups shredded carrots
¼   cup finely chopped onion
¼   cup chopped green bell pepper

Assemble all ingredients and utensils. In a jar with a lid combine the mustard, sugar substitute, oil, salt, celery seed, and vinegar. Mix or shake well and set aside.

In a mixing bowl combine the cabbage, carrots, onion, and green pepper. Pour the dressing over the vegetables and refrigerate. Yields 4 cups or 6 servings of ⅔ cup each.

Calories: 50; Fat: 2 g; Cholesterol: 0 mg; Sodium: 121 mg;
Carbohydrates: 7 g; Fiber: 0.9 g; Diabetic Exchange: 1 vegetable, ½ fat

MACARONI SALAD

8	ounces uncooked elbow macaroni
2	cups sliced celery
2	cups chopped red bell pepper
¼	cup chopped green onion
½	cup reduced-calorie mayonnaise
1	tablespoon Dijon mustard
⅓	cup light rice vinegar dressing
¼	teaspoon ground black pepper

Assemble all ingredients and utensils. Cook the macaroni according to the package directions. In a serving bowl combine the macaroni, celery, red pepper, and onion. In a separate bowl combine the mayonnaise, mustard, rice vinegar dressing, and pepper, mixing well. Pour the dressing mixture over the salad, tossing to coat the salad. Yields 8 servings of 1 cup each.

Calories: 182; Fat: 6 g; Cholesterol: 5 mg; Sodium: 378 mg;
Carbohydrates: 27 g; Fiber: 0.6 g; Diabetic Exchange: 1½ starch,
1 fat, ½ vegetable

BROWN RICE AND LENTIL SALAD

½ cup lentils, washed

1½ cups water

¾ cup quick-cooking brown rice

1 cup chopped Italian plum tomatoes

¼ cup sliced green onions

1 cup diced carrots

1 cup chopped green bell pepper

1 cup broccoli flowerets

1 tablespoon chopped fresh parsley

3 tablespoons light rice vinegar dressing

1 tablespoon lemon juice

1 teaspoon Dijon mustard

Assemble all ingredients and utensils. In a saucepan add the lentils to the water, and bring the water to a boil. Reduce the heat, cover, and simmer for 30 minutes. Drain.

In a separate pan cook the brown rice according to the package directions.

In a large bowl combine the lentils, rice, tomatoes, onions, carrots, green pepper, broccoli, and parsley. In a separate bowl mix together the rice vinegar dressing, lemon juice, and mustard. Pour the dressing mixture over the salad and refrigerate until chilled. Yields 8 servings of 1 cup each.

Calories: 65; Fat: 0.5 g; Cholesterol: 0 mg; Sodium: 181 mg; Carbohydrates: 13 g; Fiber: 2 g; Diabetic Exchange: 1 starch

SOUTHWESTERN RICE SALAD

2   cups cooked wild rice
1   cup cooked brown rice
1   cup cooked barley
1   cup soaked bulgar (cracked wheat)
½   cup toasted pecan halves, chopped
1   cup fresh corn kernels, sautéed
1   large tomato, peeled, seeded, and chopped
1   cup chopped green onions
½   cup chopped fresh parsley

Dressing:
1   cup rice vinegar
¼   cup peanut oil

Assemble all ingredients and utensils. In a serving bowl combine the rices, barley, bulgar, pecans, corn, tomato, green onions, and parsley. In a small bowl combine the ingredients for the dressing. Pour the dressing over the salad. Yields 8 servings of 1 cup per serving.

Calories: 199; Fat: 6 g; Cholesterol: 0 mg; Sodium: 285 mg;
Carbohydrates: 32 g; Fiber: 0.9 g; Diabetic Exchange: 2 starch, 1 fat

PASTA SALAD WITH SESAME DRESSING

8   ounces dry eggless pasta shells
¼   cup broccoli flowerets

Dressing:

1   tablespoon tahini (sesame butter)
1   teaspoon sesame oil
¼   cup defatted or nonfat chicken stock
2   tablespoons white wine vinegar
1   tablespoon low-sodium soy sauce

¼   cup green bell pepper strips
¼   cup red bell pepper strips
2   tablespoons chopped green onion
¼   cup sliced water chestnuts
1   teaspoon toasted sesame seeds

Assemble all ingredients and utensils. Cook the pasta in boiling water until al dente. Drain, rinse, and set aside. Steam the broccoli until tender but still green in color.

In a blender combine the ingredients for the dressing. Process until smooth. In a large bowl toss the dressing with the pasta, vegetables, and sesame seeds. Refrigerate. Yields 4 servings of 1 cup each.

Calories: 260; Fat: 5 g; Cholesterol: 0 mg; Sodium: 157 mg; Carbohydrates: 46 g; Fiber: 0.3 g; Diabetic Exchange: 3 starch, 1 fat

BARLEY PECAN SALAD

⅔   cup water
1   cup quick-cooking barley
1   cup chopped celery
½   cup finely chopped green onions
⅓   cup chopped fresh parsley

¼   cup plain nonfat yogurt

¼   cup wine vinegar, red or white

1   tablespoon prepared mustard

¼   teaspoon freshly ground black pepper

2   11-ounce cans mandarin orange segments, drained

⅓   cup coarsely chopped pecans

Assemble all ingredients and utensils. In a large saucepan bring the water to a boil. Stir in the barley and reduce the heat. Cover and simmer for 10 to 15 minutes. Remove the pan from the heat and let the barley sit for several minutes. Rinse the barley. In a large bowl combine the barley and the remaining ingredients. Yields 8 servings of ¾ cup each.

Calories: 166; Fat: 3 g; Cholesterol: 0.2 g; Sodium: 47 mg; Carbohydrates: 33 g; Fiber: 0.2 g; Diabetic Exchange: 1 starch, 1 fat, 1 fruit

CHICKEN AND ARTICHOKE SALAD

½   pound skinless, boneless chicken breasts, cooked and chopped

1   8-ounce can artichoke hearts, packed in water, drained

1   small red bell pepper, sliced in thin strips

1   rib celery, diced

¼   cup minced red onion

1   cup cooked long-grain brown rice

1   tablespoon dried leaf tarragon

½   cup low-fat red wine vinaigrette dressing

Assemble all ingredients and utensils. In a large bowl combine the chicken, vegetables, rice, and tarragon. Pour on the dressing and toss. Refrigerate several hours. Yields 6 servings.

Calories: 104; Fat: 0.8 g; Cholesterol: 23 mg; Sodium: 51 mg; Carbohydrates: 14 g; Fiber: 1 g; Diabetic Exchange: 1 lower fat meat, ½ starch, 1 vegetable

CHICKEN AND BROWN RICE SALAD

2   cups cubed cooked chicken breast
1½   cups cooked brown rice
½   cup pecans, coarsely chopped
1   small red onion, chopped
1   celery stalk, chopped
½   cup nonfat mayonnaise
1   tablespoon lemon juice
¼   teaspoon white pepper
½   teaspoon leaf thyme
½   teaspoon leaf basil
        Lettuce
        Parsley for garnish

Assemble all ingredients and utensils. In a medium bowl mix the chicken, rice, pecans, onion, and celery. In a separate bowl combine the mayonnaise, lemon juice, pepper, thyme, and basil. Add the dressing to the chicken mixture and mix well. Serve on lettuce and garnish with fresh parsley. Yields 6 servings of ½ cup each.

Calories: 222; Fat: 8.6 g; Cholesterol: 40 mg; Sodium: 183 mg; Carbohydrates: 18.8 g; Fiber: 0.5 g; Diabetic Exchange: 2 lower fat meat, 1 starch, 1 fat

CHICKEN SALAD WITH GRAPES

Great served in a cantaloupe or pineapple shell.

2   *tablespoons reduced-calorie mayonnaise*

2   *tablespoons plain nonfat yogurt*

½   *teaspoon cinnamon*

⅛   *teaspoon salt*

2   *cups cooked, chopped chicken breast*

½   *cup sliced celery*

1   *cup seedless grapes, white or red*

Assemble all ingredients and utensils. In a large bowl combine the mayonnaise, yogurt, cinnamon, and salt, and mix well. Add the chicken, celery, and grapes, and toss to coat. Refrigerate. Yields 4 servings of 1 cup each.

Calories: 144; Fat: 3.9 g; Cholesterol: 58 mg; Sodium: 141 mg; Carbohydrates: 5.7 g; Fiber: 0.3 g; Diabetic Exchange: 3 lower fat meat

TACO SALAD

1   pound lean ground beef
1   medium onion, chopped
1   tablespoon chili powder
½   teaspoon ground cumin
¼   teaspoon garlic powder
⅛   teaspoon ground oregano
⅛   teaspoon ground red pepper
1   14½-ounce can Mexican-style diced tomatoes, undrained
6   cups torn iceberg and romaine lettuce
    Chopped red pepper, yellow pepper, and green onions for garnish
    Tortilla chips (optional)

Assemble all ingredients and utensils. In a large nonstick skillet brown the ground beef and onion over medium heat for 5 to 10 minutes, or until the beef is no longer pink. Drain. Stir in the seasonings and tomatoes. Simmer for 10 to 15 minutes, stirring occasionally.

To serve, divide the lettuce among 4 plates and top each with ¼ of the beef mixture. Sprinkle with peppers. Sprinkle with tortilla chips if desired. Yields 4 servings of ¾ cup each.

Calories: 252; Fat: 13 g; Cholesterol: 70 mg; Sodium: 578 mg; Carbohydrates: 11 g; Fiber: 28 g; Diabetic Exchange: 2 vegetable, 3 lower fat meat

SOUTHWESTERN CRAB MEAT SALAD

4 6-inch tortillas formed into bowls
½ pound cooked lump crab meat
½ cup diced tomato
⅓ cup chopped green bell pepper
¼ cup chopped green onion
1 tablespoon chopped fresh cilantro
1½ tablespoons lime juice
1 small clove garlic, minced
1 teaspoon ground black pepper
⅛ teaspoon salt
1 cup shredded romaine lettuce

Assemble all ingredients and utensils. Place the tortillas on a large baking sheet. Bake at 350° 15 minutes or until crisp.

In a medium bowl combine the crab meat, tomato, green pepper, onion, and cilantro. Mix well. Stir in the lime juice, garlic, pepper, and salt.

To serve, fill each tortilla with ¼ cup of shredded lettuce and ½ cup of crab mixture. Yields 4 servings of ½ cup each.

Calories: 134; Fat: 2 g; Cholesterol: 30 mg; Sodium: 683 mg; Carbohydrates: 16 g; Fiber: 0.7 g; Diabetic Exchange: 1 lower fat meat, 1 starch, ½ vegetable

CURRIED TUNA SALAD

2   6½-ounce cans water-packed tuna, drained
1   8-ounce can sliced water chestnuts, drained
¼   cup reduced-calorie mayonnaise
1   tablespoon chopped red onion
1   tablespoon lemon juice
2   teaspoons low-sodium soy sauce
1   teaspoon curry powder

Assemble all ingredients and utensils. In a medium bowl combine all of the ingredients and mix well. Refrigerate. Yields 4 servings of ¾ cup each.

Calories: 193; Fat: 6 g; Cholesterol: 22 mg; Sodium: 619 mg;
Carbohydrates: 6 g; Fiber: 0.2 g; Diabetic Exchange: 3 lower fat meat,
1 vegetable, 1 fat

RASPBERRY VINAIGRETTE

½   cup raspberry vinegar
½   cup canned low-sodium chicken broth, undiluted
1   packet sugar substitute
1   teaspoon olive oil
⅛   teaspoon salt
⅛   teaspoon freshly ground black pepper

Assemble all ingredients and utensils. In a small jar combine all of the ingredients. Cover tightly and shake to mix. Refrigerate. Yields 1 cup or 12 servings of 1 tablespoon each.

Calories: 5; Fat: 0.4 g; Cholesterol: 0 mg; Sodium: 23 mg;
Carbohydrates: 1 g; Fiber: 0 g; Diabetic Exchange: free

BALSAMIC VINAIGRETTE

1   tablespoon Dijon mustard
¼   cup balsamic vinegar
2   tablespoons water
2   tablespoons fresh lemon juice
¼   teaspoon dried leaf tarragon
1   clove garlic, minced
2   tablespoons safflower oil
2   tablespoons virgin olive oil
½   teaspoon ground black pepper
¼   teaspoon salt

Assemble all ingredients and utensils. In a jar combine the mustard, vinegar, water, lemon juice, tarragon, and garlic. Shake well to combine. Slowly add the oils. Shake again. Mix in the pepper and salt. Chill before serving. Yields ¾ cup or 12 servings of 1 tablespoon each.

Calories: 44; Fat: 5 g; Cholesterol: 0 mg; Sodium: 77 mg; Carbohydrates: 0.6 g; Fiber: 0 g; Diabetic Exchange: 1 fat

BUTTERMILK MUSTARD DRESSING

½   cup buttermilk
¼   cup plain low-fat yogurt
1   tablespoon Dijon mustard
1½ tablespoons peeled, seeded, and grated cucumber
1   green onion, chopped
2   teaspoons chopped fresh parsley
1   teaspoon grated lemon zest
1   teaspoon grated orange zest
⅛   teaspoon ground white pepper

Assemble all ingredients and utensils. In a container with a cover blend all ingredients. Cover and refrigerate before serving. Yields ¾ cup or 12 servings of 1 tablespoon each.

Calories: 10; Fat: 0.2 g; Cholesterol: 0.7 mg; Sodium: 47 mg;
Carbohydrates: 1 g; Fiber: 0 g; Diabetic Exchange: free

BUTTERMILK RANCH

1   0.4-ounce package ranch-style dressing mix that calls for buttermilk
½   cup nonfat plain yogurt
½   cup nonfat mayonnaise
2   cups buttermilk

Assemble all ingredients and utensils. In a container with a lid combine the dressing mix package with the yogurt and mayonnaise. Mix in the buttermilk. Store in the covered container in the refrigerator. Yields 3 cups or 48 servings of 1 tablespoon each.

Calories: 8; Fat: 0.1 g; Cholesterol: 0.4 mg; Sodium: 61 mg;
Carbohydrates: 1 g; Fiber: 0 g; Diabetic Exchange: free

GINGER YOGURT DRESSING

½   cup plain nonfat yogurt
2   tablespoons fresh lemon juice
1   teaspoon safflower oil
1   tablespoon apple juice
2   teaspoons grated fresh ginger
½   cup plain nonfat yogurt
1   teaspoon honey

Assemble all ingredients and utensils. Combine all of the ingredients in a container with a cover and mix well. Refrigerate. Yields ¾ cup or 12 servings of 1 tablespoon each.

Calories: 12; Fat: 0.4 g; Cholesterol: 0.2 mg; Sodium: 6 mg;
Carbohydrates: 2 g; Fiber: 0 g; Diabetic Exchange: free

POPPY SEED DRESSING

1   cup nonfat yogurt
1   tablespoon honey
1   tablespoon lemon juice
1   teaspoon poppy seeds

Assemble all ingredients and utensils. In a container with a cover combine all of the ingredients and mix well. Store in the refrigerator. Yields 1 cup or 16 servings of 1 tablespoon each.

Calories: 12; Fat: 0.1 g; Cholesterol: 0.3 mg; Sodium: 10 mg;
Carbohydrates: 2 g; Fiber: 0 g; Diabetic Exchange: free

CREAMY GARLIC DRESSING

¼   cup nonfat yogurt
¼   cup nonfat mayonnaise
½   cup low-fat buttermilk
2   teaspoons fresh parsley, finely minced
3   cloves garlic, minced
½   teaspoon onion powder
½   teaspoon black pepper

Assemble all ingredients and utensils. In a container with a cover combine all of the ingredients and mix well. Cover and refrigerate. Yields 1 cup or 16 servings of 1 tablespoon each.

Calories: 9; Fat: 0.1 g; Cholesterol: 0.4 mg; Sodium: 37 mg;
Carbohydrates: 1 g; Fiber: 0 g; Diabetic Exchange: free

PESTO DRESSING OR SAUCE

1   pound fresh spinach, stems removed
½   cup plain low-fat yogurt
½   cup low-fat cottage cheese
¼   cup grated Parmesan cheese
2   tablespoons dried leaf basil
¼   cup slivered almonds, chopped
2   cloves garlic
⅓   cup fresh parsley, stems removed

Assemble all ingredients and utensils. Steam the spinach for 2 minutes. Drain. In a food processor or blender combine the spinach and remaining ingredients and process until smooth. Store in a covered container in the refrigerator. Yields 2 cups or 32 servings of 1 tablespoon each.

Calories: 17; Fat: 0.8 g; Cholesterol: 1 mg; Sodium: 40 mg; Carbohydrates: 1 g; Fiber: 0.5 g; Diabetic Exchange: free

BLUE CHEESE DRESSING

1   *ounce blue cheese*
2   *tablespoons nonfat mayonnaise*
1   *tablespoon lemon juice*
2   *tablespoons low-fat cottage cheese*
¼   *cup low-fat buttermilk*
¼   *cup plain nonfat yogurt*
⅛   *teaspoon dill*
⅛   *teaspoon garlic powder*
⅛   *teaspoon ground white pepper*

Assemble all ingredients and utensils. In a blender combine all of the ingredients and process for 30 seconds. Refrigerate. Yields 1 cup or 16 servings of 1 tablespoon each.

Calories: 12; Fat: 0.6 g; Cholesterol: 2 mg; Sodium: 52 mg; Carbohydrates: 9 g; Fiber: 0 g; Diabetic Exchange: free

SPICY TOMATO DRESSING

1   8-ounce can tomato sauce
½   teaspoon garlic salt
½   cup white vinegar
1   teaspoon dill
⅓   teaspoon Tabasco sauce
2   tablespoons grated onion
3   packets sugar substitute

Assemble all ingredients and utensils. In a blender or food processor combine all of the ingredients. Refrigerate. Yields 1½ cups or 12 servings of 2 tablespoons each.

Calories: 9; Fat: 0.1 g; Cholesterol: 0 mg; Sodium: 213 mg; Carbohydrates: 2 g; Fiber: 0.1 g; Diabetic Exchange: free

SWEET AND SOUR DRESSING

¾   cup plain nonfat yogurt
¼   cup nonfat mayonnaise
3   tablespoons apple cider vinegar
1   packet sugar substitute
1   teaspoon grated onion
½   teaspoon celery seeds
½   teaspoon dry mustard
¼   teaspoon paprika

Assemble all ingredients and utensils. In a small bowl combine all of the ingredients. Cover and refrigerate. Yields 1 cup or 12 servings of 1 tablespoon each.

Calories: 12; Fat: 0 g; Cholesterol: 0.3 mg; Sodium: 45 mg; Carbohydrates: 2 g; Fiber: 0 g; Diabetic Exchange: free

10

BREADS

APPLE RAISIN MUFFINS

2   cups all-purpose flour
2   teaspoons baking powder
½   teaspoon baking soda
1½ teaspoons cinnamon
2   teaspoons sugar
1   egg
3   tablespoons safflower oil
½   cup unsweetened apple juice
1   cup unsweetened applesauce
¼   cup raisins
½   cup coarsely chopped pecans

Assemble all ingredients and utensils. Preheat the oven to 350°. Spray 12 muffin cups with nonstick cooking spray. In a large mixing bowl combine all of the ingredients, mixing until just blended. Spoon the batter into the prepared muffin cups. Bake at 350° for 20 to 25 minutes. Yields 12 medium muffins.

Calories: 170; Fat: 7g; Cholesterol: 23 mg; Sodium: 100 mg;
Carbohydrates: 23 grams; Fiber: 0.3 g; Diabetic Exchange: 1 fat, 1 starch, ½ fruit

CARROT RAISIN MUFFINS

1   cup all-purpose flour
⅓   cup sugar
2   teaspoons baking powder
1   teaspoon ground cinnamon
¼   teaspoon salt
1   cup bran cereal
½   cup raisins
1½ cups grated carrots
¼   cup safflower oil
1   egg
½   cup skim milk

Assemble all ingredients and utensils. Preheat the oven to 400°. Line 9 muffin cups with paper liners. In a large bowl combine the flour, sugar, baking powder, cinnamon, salt, bran cereal, and raisins. Add the carrots, oil, egg, and milk. Mix just until the ingredients are moistened. Spoon the batter into the prepared muffin cups. Bake at 400° for 20 minutes, until browned or a toothpick inserted in the center comes out clean. Cool before removing the muffins from the pan. Yields 9 muffins.

Calories: 203; Fat: 7 g; Cholesterol: 31 mg; Sodium: 266 mg; Carbohydrates: 34 g; Fiber: 3 g; Diabetic Exchange: 1 starch, 1 fat

GEORGIA PEACH MUFFINS

2 tablespoons safflower oil
½ cup apple juice concentrate
2 egg whites
⅓ cup nonfat plain yogurt
¼ granulated fructose
2 cups all-purpose flour
½ cup oat bran
1 teaspoon baking soda
¼ teaspoon salt
1 cup finely chopped fresh peaches
⅓ cup chopped pecans

Assemble all ingredients and utensils. Preheat the oven to 350°. Spray 16 muffin cups with nonstick cooking spray. In a large bowl combine the oil, apple juice concentrate, egg whites, and yogurt. Mix well. In a separate bowl combine the fructose, flour, oat bran, soda, and salt. Stir the dry ingredients into the liquid mixture. Mix well. Fold in the peaches and pecans. Spoon the batter into the prepared muffin tins. Bake at 350° for 20 to 25 minutes. Yields 16 muffins.

Calories: 128; Fat: 4 g; Cholesterol: 0.1 mg; Sodium: 98 mg; Carbohydrates: 22 g; Fiber: 0.5 g; Diabetic Exchange: 1½ starch, ½ fat

HONEY BANANA MUFFINS

1   cups all-purpose flour
2   cups whole wheat pastry flour
2   teaspoons baking soda
¼   teaspoon salt
¼   teaspoon ground nutmeg
½   cup honey
1½ cups buttermilk
⅓   cup safflower oil
3   egg whites, beaten to a soft peak
3   small ripe bananas, mashed (about 1⅓ cups)

Assemble all ingredients and utensils. Preheat the oven to 350°. Spray 18 muffin cups with nonstick cooking spray. In a medium bowl sift together the dry ingredients. In a separate bowl blend together the honey, buttermilk, and oil. Gently stir in the egg whites. Add the mashed bananas. Slowly mix in the dry ingredients just until the mixture is moistened but somewhat lumpy. Pour the batter into the prepared muffin cups. Bake at 350° for 25 to 30 minutes. Yields 18 muffins.

Calories: 160; Fat: 5 g; Cholesterol: 1 mg; Sodium: 152 mg;
Carbohydrates: 28 g; Fiber: 0.5 g; Diabetic Exchange: 1½ starch, 1 fat

MORNING GLORY MUFFINS

2   *tablespoons safflower oil*
½   *cup plain nonfat yogurt*
½   *cup frozen apple juice concentrate*
¼   *cup pineapple juice*
1   *egg white*
1   *teaspoon vanilla extract*
2   *cups all-purpose flour*
¼   *cup granulated fructose*
2   *teaspoons baking powder*
½   *teaspoon baking soda*
⅛   *teaspoon salt*
1   *small can unsweetened crushed pineapple and juice*
½   *cup raw shredded carrots*
⅓   *cup chopped pecans*

Assemble all ingredients and utensils. Preheat the oven to 350°. Spray 18 muffin cups with nonstick cooking spray. In a large bowl combine the oil, yogurt, apple juice concentrate, pineapple juice, egg white, and vanilla. Mix well. Add the flour, fructose, baking powder, soda, and salt. Mix again. Fold in the pineapple with juice, carrots, and pecans. Spoon the batter into the prepared muffin cups. Bake at 350° for 15 to 20 minutes. Yields 18 muffins.

Calories: 110; Fat: 3 g; Cholesterol: 0.1 mg; Sodium: 88 mg; Carbohydrates: 19 g; Fiber: 0.1 g; Diabetic Exchange: 1 starch, ½ fat

FRESH BLUEBERRY MUFFINS

2   cups whole wheat pastry flour
1   teaspoon baking soda
1¼ cups buttermilk
2   egg whites, lightly beaten
⅓   cup honey
⅓   cup safflower oil
1   cup fresh blueberries

Assemble all ingredients and utensils. Preheat the oven to 350°. Spray 12 muffin cups with nonstick cooking spray. In a medium bowl sift together the flour and baking soda. In separate bowl whisk the buttermilk, egg whites, honey, and oil until creamy. Stir in the blueberries. Slowly mix in the dry ingredients just until the mixture is moistened but remains somewhat lumpy. Pour the batter into the prepared muffin cups. Bake at 350° for 25 to 30 minutes. Yields 12 medium muffins.

Calories: 168; Fat: 7 g; Cholesterol: 1 mg; Sodium: 105 mg; Carbohydrates: 25 g; Fiber: 0.7 g; Diabetic Exchange: 1½ starch, 1 fat

OAT BRAN MUFFINS

2¼ cups oat bran
¼   cup firmly packed brown sugar
2   teaspoons cinnamon
1   tablespoon baking powder
1   banana, mashed
1   small cooking apple, grated
2   tablespoons raisins
¼   cup egg substitute, equal to 1 egg
¾   cup orange juice
½   cup skim milk
2   tablespoons safflower oil

Assemble all ingredients and utensils. Preheat the oven to 425°. Spray 12 muffin cups with nonstick cooking spray. In a medium bowl mix the oat bran, brown sugar, cinnamon, and baking powder. Set aside. In separate bowl combine the banana, apple, raisins, egg substitute, orange juice, milk, and oil. Add the dry ingredients and mix just until moistened. Pour the batter into the prepared muffin cups. Bake at 425° for 15 to 20 minutes. Yields 12 medium muffins.

Calories: 118; Fat: 4 g; Cholesterol: 0.2 mg; Sodium: 123 mg;
Carbohydrates: 20 g; Fiber: 3 g; Diabetic Exchange: 1 starch, 1 fat

BUTTERMILK CORN MUFFINS

1   cup yellow cornmeal
1   cup all-purpose flour
2   teaspoons baking powder
½   teaspoon salt
½   teaspoon baking soda
1   tablespoon apple juice concentrate
1¼ cups nonfat buttermilk
3   tablespoons safflower oil
3   egg whites, lightly beaten

Assemble all ingredients and utensils. Preheat the oven to 400°. Spray 15 muffin cups with nonstick cooking spray. In a large bowl combine the dry ingredients, mixing until well blended. In separate bowl combine the apple juice concentrate, buttermilk, oil, and egg whites, mixing well. Fold the liquid mixture into the dry ingredients. Spoon the batter into the prepared muffin cups. Bake at 400° for 12 to 15 minutes. Yields 15 muffins.

Calories: 102; Fat: 3 g; Cholesterol: 1 mg; Sodium: 177 mg;
Carbohydrates: 15 g; Fiber: 0.1 g; Diabetic Exchange: 1 starch, ½ fat

PUMPKIN MUFFINS

¼ cup safflower oil

⅔ cup apple juice concentrate

1   16-ounce can pumpkin

½ cup skim milk

3   egg whites, slightly beaten

1¾ cups all-purpose flour

⅓ cup granulated fructose

1   teaspoon baking powder

¼ teaspoon salt

1   teaspoon cinnamon

½ teaspoon pumpkin pie spice

½ teaspoon cloves

Assemble all ingredients and utensils. Preheat the oven to 350°. Spray 18 muffin cups with nonstick cooking spray. In a large bowl combine the oil, apple juice concentrate, and pumpkin. Stir until well blended. Slowly add the milk and egg whites, continuing to stir. In a separate bowl combine the dry ingredients and blend well. Fold the dry ingredients into the liquid mixture. Mix well. Spoon the batter into the prepared muffin cups. Bake at 350° for 20 to 25 minutes. Yields 18 muffins.

Calories: 117; Fat: 3 g; Cholesterol: 0.1 mg; Sodium: 68 mg; Carbohydrates: 20 g; Fiber: 0.3 g; Diabetic Exchange: 1 starch, ½ fat

RAISIN BRAN MUFFINS

1   *cup rolled oats, not instant*
¾   *cup whole-wheat flour*
¼   *cup wheat bran*
⅓   *cup raisins*
1   *teaspoon baking powder*
⅓   *cups low-fat buttermilk*
1   *tablespoon safflower oil*
1   *tablespoon honey*
1   *teaspoon vanilla extract*

Assemble all ingredients and utensils. Preheat the oven to 350°. Spray 12 muffin cups with nonstick cooking spray. In a large bowl combine the dry ingredients. In separate bowl combine the liquid ingredients. Mix together just until the dry ingredients are moistened. Spoon the batter into the prepared muffin cups. Bake at 350° for 15 to 20 minutes. Yields 12 muffins.

Calories: 91; Fat: 2 g; Cholesterol: 1 mg; Sodium: 59 mg;
Carbohydrates: 17 g; Fiber: 2 g; Diabetic Exchange: 1 starch, ½ fat

BISCUITS

1   cup all-purpose flour
1   cup whole wheat pastry flour
1   teaspoon baking powder
¼   teaspoon salt
¼   cup safflower oil
¾   cup buttermilk

Assemble all ingredients and utensils. Preheat the oven to 450°. Spray a baking sheet with nonstick cooking spray. In a large bowl sift together the dry ingredients and mix well. Make a well in the center of the dry ingredients. Pour in the oil and quickly mix together until small clumps of dough start to form. Add the buttermilk and stir vigorously. Knead the dough in the bowl until a large ball is formed. Place the dough on a floured surface and roll out to ½-inch thickness. Cut the biscuits with a biscuit cutter. Place the biscuits on the prepared baking sheet. Bake at 450° for 10 to 12 minutes. Yields 16 biscuits.

Calories: 88; Fat: 4 g; Cholesterol: 0.4 mg; Sodium: 68 mg; Carbohydrates: 12 g; Fiber: 0 g; Diabetic Exchange: 1 starch

BUTTERMILK BISCUITS

2   cups all-purpose flour
1   tablespoon baking powder
½   teaspoon salt
¼   cup reduced-calorie margarine
1   cup buttermilk

Assemble all ingredients and utensils. Preheat the oven to 375°. In a large mixing bowl combine the dry ingredients. Cut in the margarine with a pastry blender or 2 knives until the mixture resembles coarse crumbs.

Gradually pour in the buttermilk. Stir until combined, then knead quickly to make a firm dough. On a floured surface roll out the dough to ½-inch thickness. Cut the biscuits with a medium cutter. Bake at 375° for 15 to 17 minutes. Yields 12 biscuits.

Calories: 102; Fat: 2 g; Cholesterol: 0.7 mg; Sodium: 234 mg;
Carbohydrates: 17 g; Fiber: 0 g; Diabetic Exchange: 1 starch, ½ fat

POPOVERS

⅔   cup sifted all-purpose flour
⅓   cup sifted whole wheat flour
1   egg
4   egg whites
1   cup low-fat milk
1   tablespoon margarine, melted

Assemble all ingredients and utensils. Preheat the oven to 425°. Spray 6 large muffin cups with nonstick cooking spray. In a large bowl combine the all-purpose flour, whole-wheat flour, egg, egg whites, milk, and melted margarine. Mix with an electric mixer for 3 minutes, until smooth. Spoon the batter into the prepared muffin cups, filling each cup half full of batter. Bake at 425° for 20 minutes. Do not open the door!

Reduce the oven temperature to 325° and bake for an additional 20 minutes or until the crust is golden brown. Remove the popovers and serve immediately. Yields 6 popovers.

Calories: 129; Fat: 4 g; Cholesterol: 46 mg; Sodium: 90 mg;
Carbohydrates: 17 g; Fiber: 0 g; Diabetic Exchange: 1 starch, 1 fat

WHOLE WHEAT FRENCH TOAST

Serve with fresh fruit or fruit sauce.

4   egg whites
¼   cup skim milk
1   teaspoon vanilla extract
½   teaspoon cinnamon
4   slices whole wheat bread

Assemble all ingredients and utensils. In a large bowl combine the egg whites, milk, vanilla, and cinnamon. Beat lightly. Heat a nonstick griddle or heavy skillet until hot. Dip the bread slices in the liquid mixture and brown on both sides until golden. Yields 4 servings.

> Calories: 90; Fat: 0.8 g; Cholesterol: 1 mg; Sodium: 207 mg; Carbohydrates: 15 g; Fiber: 2 g; Diabetic Exchange: 1 starch

BUTTERMILK PANCAKES

¾   cup all-purpose flour
2   teaspoons baking powder
1   teaspoon apple juice concentrate
½   cup nonfat buttermilk
¼   cup egg substitute
¼   cup water
2   teaspoons reduced-calorie margarine, melted

Assemble all ingredients and utensils. In a large bowl combine the flour and baking powder. In a separate bowl combine the apple juice concentrate, buttermilk, egg substitute, water, and margarine. Mix well. Pour the mixture into the dry ingredients and stir just until the dry ingredients are moistened.

Spray a griddle with nonstick cooking spray. Heat the griddle until hot. For each pancake, spoon 2 tablespoons of batter onto the hot griddle, spreading the batter to a 4-inch circle. Turn the pancakes when the tops are covered with bubbles and the edges look browned. Yields 12 4-inch pancakes.

Calories: 41; Fat: 0.7 g; Cholesterol: 0.4 mg; Sodium: 81 mg; Carbohydrates: 7 g; Fiber: 0 g; Diabetic Exchange: ½ starch

ORANGE SCONES

3   cups all-purpose flour
4½ teaspoons baking powder
¼   teaspoon salt
¼   cup margarine
½   cup orange juice
½   cup low-fat milk

Assemble all ingredients and utensils. Preheat the oven to 450°. Spray a baking sheet with nonstick cooking spray. In a large bowl combine the flour, baking powder, and salt. Mix well. Cut in the margarine with a pastry blender or 2 knives until the mixture resembles coarse meal. Add the orange juice and milk, mixing until the dough holds together.

Place the dough on a clean floured surface and knead for about 3 minutes. Roll out the dough to ½-inch thickness. Cut into 2-inch rounds with a biscuit cutter. Place the biscuits on the prepared baking sheet. Bake at 450° for 10 to 15 minutes or until golden brown. Yields 12 scones.

Calories: 156; Fat: 4 g; Cholesterol: 0.2 mg; Sodium: 232 mg; Carbohydrates: 26 g; Fiber: 0 g; Diabetic Exchange: 1½ starch, 1 fat

DILL BREAD

1   *package active dry yeast*
⅓   *cup warm water (110°)*
1   *cup low-fat cottage cheese*
3   *tablespoons safflower oil*
2   *tablespoons apple juice concentrate*
1   *egg, beaten*
2   *teaspoons dill*
¼   *teaspoon salt*
¼   *teaspoon baking soda*
2½ *cups all-purpose flour*
1   *egg white, beaten*
    Minced fresh dill

Assemble all ingredients and utensils. In a small bowl combine the yeast and warm water, and set the mixture aside. In a large bowl combine the cottage cheese, oil, and apple juice concentrate. Mix well. Stir in the yeast-water mixture and the beaten egg. In a separate bowl combine the remaining dry ingredients. Fold the dry ingredients into the liquid mixture. Mix until a ball forms. Place the dough on a floured surface and knead for 5 to 7 minutes. Place the dough in a lightly oiled bowl and let it rise in a warm place for 1 hour.

Spray an 8 x 11-inch loaf pan with nonstick cooking spray. Shape the dough into a loaf and place it in the prepared pan. Let the dough rise again for 30 to 40 minutes. Brush lightly with the beaten egg white and sprinkle with minced fresh dill. Bake at 350° for 35 to 40 minutes. Yields 1 loaf or 14 slices.

Calories: 131; Fat: 4 g; Cholesterol: 20 mg; Sodium: 125 mg; Carbohydrates: 19 g; Fiber: 0 mg; Diabetic Exchange: 1 starch, 1 fat

MISS DAISY'S BANANA NUT BREAD

⅓ cup vegetable oil

⅓ cup sugar

1 teaspoon vanilla extract

1 egg

2 medium ripe bananas

1½ cups whole wheat flour

2 teaspoons baking powder

½ teaspoon baking soda

½ teaspoon ground cinnamon

½ cup skim milk

½ cup chopped pecans

Assemble all ingredients and utensils. Preheat the oven to 350°. Spray a 5 x 9-inch loaf pan with nonstick cooking spray. In a large mixing bowl cream together the oil, sugar, vanilla, egg, and bananas with an electric mixer. In a separate bowl combine the flour, baking powder, soda, and cinnamon. Gradually add the dry ingredients to the banana mixture alternately with the skim milk. Fold in the pecans. Pour the batter into the prepared loaf pan. Bake at 350° for 45 to 50 minutes, until browned and tests done. Yields 1 loaf or 12 ½-inch thick slices.

Calories: 184; Fat: 10 g; Cholesterol: 23 mg; Sodium: 104 mg; Carbohydrates: 22 g; Fiber: 0.8 g; Diabetic Exchange: 1 starch, 1 fat, ⅓ fruit

HERB CHEESE BREAD

1	1-pound loaf French or Italian bread
2	tablespoons melted margarine
¼	cup grated Parmesan cheese
1	tablespoon fresh minced parsley
2	cloves garlic, crushed

Assemble all ingredients and utensils. Preheat the oven to 400°. Slice the bread in half horizontally. Coat the cut surface of each half with margarine. In a small bowl combine the Parmesan cheese, parsley, and garlic. Sprinkle the mixture over the surface of half of the loaf. Top with the other half of the loaf.

Wrap the loaf in heavy duty aluminum foil. Bake at 400° for 12 to 15 minutes or until the bread is heated thoroughly. Yields 20 ½-inch slices.

Calories: 117; Fat: 3 g; Cholesterol: 2 mg; Sodium: 237 mg;
Carbohydrates: 20 g; Fiber: 0.1 g; Diabetic Exchange: 1 starch, ½ fat

FRENCH BREAD

2	packages active dry yeast
2½	cups warm water (110°)
3	tablespoons honey
6	cups whole wheat pastry flour
¾	cup nonfat dry milk powder
1	teaspoon salt or more to taste
2	tablespoons safflower oil

Assemble all ingredients and utensils. Preheat the oven to 450°. Spray a baking sheet with nonstick cooking spray. In a 1-quart bowl dissolve the yeast in ½ cup of warm water. Add the honey and set the mixture aside to allow it to bubble. In a large bowl combine all of the dry ingredients. Mix well. Add 2 cups of the water and the oil to the yeast mixture. Pour the liquid mixture into the dry ingredients. Mix until smooth. Add ½ cup of additional flour if necessary to reach kneading consistency. Knead for 3 to 4 minutes. Divide the dough in half and shape it into 2 loaves. Place the loaves on the prepared baking sheet. Cut 3 diagonal slashes across the tops and let the loaves rise. Bake at 450° for 45 minutes. Remove the loaves from the pan and cool on a rack. Yields 2 loaves, 12 slices from each loaf.

Calories: 127; Fat: 2 g; Cholesterol: 0.4 mg; Sodium: 103 mg;
Carbohydrates: 25 g; Fiber: 1 g; Diabetic Exchange: 1½ starch

GARLIC PARMESAN BREAD

1   tablespoon olive oil
2   tablespoons hot water
1   tablespoon grated Parmesan cheese
2   teaspoons dried leaf oregano
2   cloves garlic, minced
1   loaf French bread, cut into 16 slices

Assemble all ingredients and utensils. Preheat the oven to 350°. In a small bowl whisk together the oil and water. Whisk in the Parmesan, oregano, and garlic. With a pastry brush coat both sides of each bread slice with the garlic mixture. Put the slices back together and wrap the loaf in foil. Bake at 350° for 15 minutes. Yields 16 servings.

Calories: 89; Fat: 2 g; Cholesterol: 0.2 mg; Sodium: 171 mg;
Carbohydrates: 15 g; Fiber: 0 g; Diabetic Exchange: 1 starch

CHICKEN DRESSING

2   tablespoons safflower oil
1   cup finely chopped celery
½   cup finely chopped onions
2   cups fat-free chicken broth
½   teaspoon ground sage
½   teaspoon ground thyme
¼   teaspoon ground black pepper
2   egg whites
12 slices day-old white bread, cubed

Assemble all ingredients and utensils. Preheat the oven to 375°. Spray an 8-inch square pan or 1-quart casserole with nonstick cooking spray. In a saucepan heat the oil. Add the celery and onions and cook over medium heat for 5 minutes, stirring frequently. Remove the pan from the heat and add the broth and seasonings. Mix well. Add the egg whites and mix well. Pour the mixture over the bread cubes. Toss slightly. Bake at 375° for 40 to 45 minutes. Yields 12 servings.

Calories: 96; Fat: 3 g; Cholesterol: 1 mg; Sodium: 145 mg;
Carbohydrates: 14 g; Fiber: 0.1 g; Diabetic Exchange: 1 starch, ½ fat

~❧ 11 ❧~

ENTRÉES

ROASTED PORK TENDERLOIN

2   ½-pound pork tenderloins
2   tablespoons Dijon mustard
1   cup breadcrumbs
1   tablespoon rubbed sage
1   clove garlic, minced
¼   teaspoon ground black pepper

Assemble all ingredients and utensils. Preheat the oven to 400°. Spray a shallow roasting pan with nonstick cooking spray. Trim any fat from the tenderloins. Place the tenderloins on a rack in the prepared pan. Brush the tenderloins evenly with mustard. In a small bowl combine the breadcrumbs and remaining ingredients. Rub the mixture over the tenderloins. Bake at 400° for 35 to 40 minutes or until a meat thermometer registers 160 degrees. Yields 6 servings of 2 ounces each.

Calories: 202; Fat: 0 g; Cholesterol: 54 mg; Sodium: 226 mg;
Carbohydrates: 10 g; Fiber: 0 g; Diabetic Exchange: 2 lower fat meat, 1 starch

PORK CHOPS WITH ROSEMARY

Great served with rice.

4   pork loin chops, about ½-inch thick
½   teaspoon ground black pepper
2   green onions, chopped
½   cup dry sherry
1½ teaspoons crumbled dried leaf rosemary

Assemble all ingredients and utensils. Spray a nonstick skillet with non-stick cooking spray. Trim the fat from the pork chops. Brown the pork chops on both sides in the prepared skillet. Sprinkle with pepper and add the onions, sherry, and rosemary. Cover and simmer over low heat for 20 to 25 minutes, until the meat is tender. Yields 4 servings.

Calories: 214; Fat: 7 g; Cholesterol: 70 mg; Sodium: 61 mg;
Carbohydrates: 4 g; Fiber: 0 g; Diabetic Exchange: 3 medium fat meat, 1 fat

PORK CHOPS IN ORANGE GINGER SAUCE

4   medium pork chops
1   medium yellow onion, sliced thin
½   cup orange juice
2   teaspoons honey
½   teaspoon ground ginger
⅛   teaspoon ground cloves
    Orange slices for garnish

Assemble all ingredients and utensils. In a nonstick skillet brown the pork chops on both sides with the onions over medium high heat. Add the orange juice, honey, ginger, and cloves. Cover and cook over medium heat for 45 to 50 minutes or until the pork chops are tender. Garnish with orange slices. Yields 4 servings.

Calories: 200; Fat: 7 g; Cholesterol: 70 mg; Sodium: 61 mg;
Carbohydrates: 8 g; Fiber: 0.2 g; Diabetic Exchange: 3 high fat meat, ½ starch

MISS DAISY'S MEAT LOAF

1   pound ground round
1   cup oats, uncooked
½   cup minced onion
¼   cup minced green bell pepper
2   egg whites, slightly beaten
½   teaspoon salt
½   teaspoon ground black pepper
1   teaspoon Worcestershire sauce
¾   cup tomato sauce

Assemble all ingredients and utensils. Preheat the oven to 400°. In a large bowl combine all of the ingredients except one-fourth of the tomato sauce. Shape into a large loaf or 2 mini loaves and place them in loaf pans. Spread the remaining tomato sauce over each loaf. Bake at 400° for 40 to 45 minutes. Yields 6 servings of 2 ounces each.

Calories: 145; Fat: 6 g; Cholesterol: 36 mg; Sodium: 316 mg;
Carbohydrates: 10 g; Fiber: 1 g; Diabetic Exchange: 2 medium fat meat, ½ starch

PEPPER STEAK

3 tablespoons black peppercorns
1 pound beef flank steak
1½ teaspoons olive oil

Assemble all ingredients and utensils. Preheat the broiler. Crack the peppercorns in a food processor. Trim any fat from the steak. Brush the steak with oil and sprinkle with peppercorns on both sides. Place on a broiler pan and cook 3 inches under the broiler for 4 to 5 minutes. Turn and broil for 4 more minutes. Remove the steak from the broiler and thinly slice diagonally, across the grain. Yields 4 servings of 3 ounces each.

Calories: 195; Fat: 10 g; Cholesterol: 57 mg; Sodium: 71 mg;
Carbohydrates: 1 g; Fiber: 0 g; Diabetic Exchange: 3 meat

MISS DAISY'S POT ROAST

1 4-pound round roast, fat removed
1 teaspoon ground black pepper
1 teaspoon dried leaf oregano
1 teaspoon dried leaf thyme
2 cloves garlic, crushed
1 bay leaf
2 medium onions, chopped
2 large carrots, cut into large chunks
1 cup tomato purée
1 cup dry red wine or low-sodium beef stock

Assemble all ingredients and utensils. Preheat the oven to 325°. In a non-stick skillet brown the roast. Transfer the roast to a Dutch oven or large roasting pan. Sprinkle with pepper, oregano, and thyme. In a medium bowl combine the crushed garlic, bay leaf, onions, carrots, and tomato purée. Spread the mixture over the roast. Pour red wine or beef stock over the entire roast. Cover tightly. Bake at 325° for 2 hours and 30 minutes to 3 hours, or until the meat is tender. Discard the bay leaf. Yields 8 servings of 4 ounces each.

Calories: 343; Fat: 11 g; Cholesterol: 109 mg; Sodium: 231 mg;
Carbohydrates: 8 g; Fiber: 0.5 g; Diabetic Exchange: 6 meat, 1 vegetable

GRILLED ONION BURGERS

¼   cup dry white wine
2   tablespoons chopped fresh basil
½   cup chopped onion
1   pound lean ground beef
4   whole wheat buns

Assemble all ingredients and utensils. In a medium bowl combine the wine, basil, onion, and beef. Refrigerate for 1 hour or more. Form into 4 burger patties and grill or fry to the desired degree of doneness. Serve on whole wheat buns with condiments. Yields 4 servings of 3 ounces each.

Calories: 344 (with bun); Fat: 15 g; Cholesterol: 68 mg; Sodium: 306 mg;
Carbohydrates: 23 g; Fiber: 2 g; Diabetic Exchange: 3 lower fat meat, 1½ starch

TENDERLOIN POT ROAST

¼ cup soy sauce

1 tablespoon Worcestershire sauce

1 clove garlic

1 3-pound beef tenderloin roast

2 onions, quartered

½ pound fresh mushrooms, sliced

3 ribs celery, sliced

3 carrots, peeled and sliced

¼ cup water

4 to 6 small new potatoes, halved

Assemble all ingredients and utensils. In a large dish combine the soy sauce, Worcestershire sauce, and garlic. Marinate the tenderloin overnight in the mixture.

In a roasting pot arrange the marinated tenderloin, onions, mushrooms, celery, carrots, and water. Bake, covered, at 325° for 2 hours and 30 minutes. Add the potatoes and bake another 30 minutes. Yields 12 servings of 3 ounces each plus divided vegetables.

Calories: 230; Fat: 10 g; Cholesterol: 73 mg; Sodium: 363 mg; Carbohydrates: 10 g; Fiber: 0.5 g; Diabetic Exchange: 3 medium fat meat, ½ starch

VEAL PARMESAN

1   *pound veal leg round steak*
½   *cup chopped onion*
1   *clove garlic, minced*
¼   *cup chopped green bell pepper*
1   *tablespoon olive oil*
2   *tablespoons freshly grated Parmesan cheese*
1   *cup tomato sauce*
1   *tablespoon dry red or white wine*
2   *ounces freshly shredded part-skim mozzarella cheese*

Assemble all ingredients and utensils. Cut the veal into 6 3-ounce pieces. Pound each piece to ¼-inch thickness. In a large skillet cook the onion, garlic, and green pepper in oil until tender. Push the mixture to one side of the skillet; add the veal and brown on both sides.

In a small bowl combine the Parmesan cheese, tomato sauce, and wine. Pour the mixture over the meat. Cover and cook over low heat for 20 to 25 minutes or until the meat is tender.

Sprinkle the mozzarella cheese over the meat and sauce. Cover and heat for 5 minutes or until the cheese is melted. Yields 6 servings of 3 ounces each.

Calories: 276; Fat: 12 g; Cholesterol: 110 mg; Sodium: 560 mg; Carbohydrates: 7 g; Fiber: 0.2 g; Diabetic Exchange: 1 lower fat meat, 1 vegetable, 1 fat

SWISS STEAK

1   *2-pound round steak*
1   *teaspoon minced garlic*
½   *teaspoon ground black pepper*
1   *16-ounce can chopped tomatoes with juice*
1   *small onion, chopped*
1   *medium green bell pepper, seeded and sliced*
1   *cup sliced mushrooms*

Assemble all ingredients and utensils. Preheat the oven to 350°. Tenderize the round steak with a meat tenderizer or have the butcher take care of this for you. Place the round steak in a deep baking pan. Sprinkle with garlic and pepper. Add the remaining ingredients. Cover and bake at 350° for 50 to 55 minutes. Remove the cover and cook for another 15 minutes or until tender. Yields 6 servings of 4 ounces per person.

Calories: 222; Fat: 9 g; Cholesterol: 81 mg; Sodium: 233 mg; Carbohydrates: 8 g; Fiber: 0.6 g; Diabetic Exchange: 4 lower fat meat, 1 vegetable

CHICKEN OR TURKEY RICE CASSEROLE

1   *4-ounce can mushroom stems and pieces*
1   *10¾-ounce can cream of chicken soup, low sodium*
½   *cup fat-free chicken broth*
1   *cup diced cooked chicken or turkey breast*
½   *cup long-grain rice*
½   *teaspoon chopped parsley*

Assemble all ingredients and utensils. Preheat the oven to 325°. In a saucepan combine the mushrooms, soup, and broth. Cook, stirring constantly, over medium heat until smooth and bubbling.

Add the chicken, rice, and parsley to the hot soup mixture. Mix well and transfer a 1½- to 2-quart casserole. Cover tightly. Bake at 325° for 45 minutes. Yields 3 cups or 4 servings of ¾ cup each.

Calories: 194; Fat: 3 g; Cholesterol: 34 mg; Sodium: 444 mg; Carbohydrates: 28 g; Fiber: 0.1 g; Diabetic Exchange: 2 starch, 1 lower fat meat

MISS DAISY'S CHICKEN OR TURKEY DIVAN

4   *cups broccoli flowerets*
1¼ *cups Cheese Sauce (see recipe, p. 229)*
½   *teaspoon curry powder*
2   *cups chopped cooked low-fat turkey or chicken*
2   *tablespoons grated Parmesan cheese*
2   *tablespoons whole wheat low-fat breadcrumbs*
1   *tablespoon slivered almonds*

Assemble all ingredients and utensils. Preheat the oven to 350°. Steam, boil or blanch the broccoli for 2 to 3 minutes. Drain. Prepare the Cheese Sauce. Add curry powder and mix well. In a 2-quart casserole layer the broccoli, chicken or turkey, and Cheese Sauce, and repeat the layers. Top with Parmesan cheese, breadcrumbs, and almonds. Bake at 350° for 20 minutes or until heated. Yields 8 servings of 4 ounces each.

Calories: 120; Fat: 4 g; Cholesterol: 26 mg; Sodium: 140 mg; Carbohydrates: 6 g; Fiber: 0.6 g; Diabetic Exchange: 1½ lower fat meat, ½ vegetable

APRICOT CHICKEN

4   4-ounce skinless, boneless chicken breasts
¼   cup low-calorie French dressing
3   tablespoons low-sugar apricot jam
1   tablespoon dried onion flakes
2   tablespoons water

Assemble all ingredients and utensils. Preheat the oven to 350°. Spray a baking pan with nonstick cooking spray. Arrange the chicken in the prepared pan. Bake, uncovered, at 350° for 20 to 25 minutes. In a small bowl combine the remaining ingredients and pour the mixture over the chicken breasts. Bake for another 10 to 15 minutes or until the chicken is done and the sauce heated. Yields 4 servings of 4 ounces each.

Calories: 165; Fat: 4 g; Cholesterol: 68 mg; Sodium: 391 mg; Carbohydrates: 5 g; Fiber: 0 g; Diabetic Exchange: ½ fat, 4 lower fat meat

DIJON CHICKEN BREASTS

1   tablespoon safflower oil
½   cup all-purpose flour
1   teaspoon paprika
4   5-ounce skinless, boneless chicken breasts
1   cup defatted or low-fat chicken broth
2   tablespoons Dijon mustard
4   cloves garlic, minced
2   green onions, finely chopped
     Fresh parsley sprigs for garnish

Assemble all ingredients and utensils. Preheat the oven to 350°. Oil an ovenproof baking dish. In a medium bowl combine the flour and paprika. Dredge or coat the chicken breasts in the flour mixture one at a time.

Arrange the chicken breasts in the prepared dish. Bake at 350° for 25 minutes.

In a separate bowl blend the chicken broth with the mustard and garlic. Pour the broth mixture over the chicken breasts and sprinkle with green onions. Bake for another 25 minutes, until done. Garnish with fresh parsley sprigs. Yields 4 servings of 4 ounces each.

Calories: 271; Fat: 6 g; Cholesterol: 86 mg; Sodium: 293; Carbohydrates: 14 g; Fiber: 0 g; Diabetic Exchange: 1 starch, 5 lower fat meat

GINGER CHICKEN

4   4-ounce skinless, boneless chicken breasts
1   teaspoon ginger
1   teaspoon safflower oil
4   green onions, finely chopped
1   clove garlic, finely chopped
2   tablespoons low-sodium soy sauce
2   tablespoons water

Assemble all ingredients and utensils. Preheat the oven to 350°. Arrange the chicken breasts in a shallow baking pan. Bake at 350° for 10 minutes.

In a small bowl combine the remaining ingredients for ginger sauce. Pour the sauce over the chicken breasts. Bake for an additional 20 minutes or until done. Yields 4 servings of 3 ounces each.

Calories: 149; Fat: 3 g; Cholesterol: 68 mg; Sodium: 377 mg; Carbohydrates: 2 g; Fiber: 0 g; Diabetic Exchange: 4 lower fat meat

MISS DAISY'S SWEET AND SOUR CHICKEN

Serve over brown rice.

1   *pound boneless, skinless chicken breasts*
1   *8-ounce can unsweetened pineapple chunks, drained, reserving the juice*
1   *cup low-fat chicken broth*
¼   *cup vinegar*
1   *teaspoon soy sauce*
⅛   *teaspoon garlic powder*
1   *cup diced celery*
1   *small onion, quartered*
1   *medium green bell pepper, sliced*
3   *tablespoons cornstarch*
¼   *cup water*
5   *packets sugar substitute*

Assemble all ingredients and utensils. Cut the chicken into bite-size pieces. In a saucepan combine the chicken, reserved juice, broth, vinegar, soy sauce, and garlic powder. Cover and simmer for 15 minutes. Add the pineapple chunks and vegetables. Cook for another 15 minutes, stirring often. In a small bowl combine the cornstarch and water. Gradually stir the cornstarch mixture into the hot chicken mixture. Cook until thickened. Stir in the sugar substitute. Yields 6 servings of ¾ cup each.

Calories: 141; Fat: 1 g; Cholesterol: 46 mg; Sodium: 127 mg; Carbohydrates: 14 g; Fiber: 0.6 g; Diabetic Exchange: 2 lower fat meat, 1 starch

MISS DAISY'S CREAMED CHICKEN

1   *4-ounce can mushroom stems and pieces*
2   *tablespoons safflower oil*
3   *cups fat-free, low-sodium chicken broth*
3   *tablespoons cornstarch*
¼   *cup nonfat dry milk*
⅛   *teaspoon white pepper*
2   *cups chopped cooked chicken breast*
¼   *cup chopped drained pimiento*
¼   *cup drained sliced water chestnuts*

Assemble all ingredients and utensils. Drain the mushrooms well and discard the juice. In a saucepan heat the oil and sauté the mushrooms over medium heat until the mushrooms are lightly browned.

Mix together the broth, cornstarch, dry milk, and pepper until smooth. Add the mixture all at once to the mushrooms and cook over moderate heat until thickened. Continue to cook and stir for 3 more minutes. Add the chicken, pimiento, and water chestnuts to the sauce and mix lightly. Cook until warmed through. Serve over low-fat, low-calorie toast points. Yields 8 servings of 1/2 cup each.

Calories: 120; Fat: 5 g; Cholesterol: 30 mg; Sodium: 84 mg;
Carbohydrates: 6 g; Fiber: 0.2 g; Diabetic Exchange: 1 lower fat meat, ½ milk

BARBECUED CHICKEN

4   *6-ounce boneless, skinless chicken breast halves*
½   *cup jellied cranberry sauce*
¼   *cup no-salt-added tomato paste*
2   *tablespoons prepared mustard*
1   *teaspoon apple cider vinegar*

Assemble all ingredients and utensils. Preheat the oven to 350°. Place the chicken breasts in a 2-quart baking dish. In a mixer combine the cranberry sauce, tomato paste, mustard, and apple cider vinegar. Mix until smooth. Brush the mixture over both sides of the chicken. Reserve the remaining mixture. Cover the dish. Bake at 350° for 30 minutes. Remove the cover, turn the chicken, and brush with the remaining cranberry mixture. Bake, uncovered, for an additional 20 minutes or until the chicken is tender. Yields 4 servings.

Calories: 261; Fat: 2.3 g; Cholesterol: 103 mg; Sodium: 225 mg; Carbohydrates: 15 g; Fiber: 0 g; Diabetic Exchange: 6 lower fat meat, 1 fruit

ROASTED CHICKEN WITH COUSCOUS

1   10-ounce package couscous
¼   cup apricot preserves
1   3-pound skinless roasted chicken from supermarket deli, quartered
½   cup water
1   pound medium carrots, peeled and cut into ¼-inch diagonal slices (about 1½ cups)
¼   cup chopped green onions
     Freshly ground black pepper to taste

Assemble all ingredients and utensils. Preheat the oven to 425°. Line a baking pan with aluminum foil. Prepare the couscous according to the package directions. Arrange the chicken in the foil-lined pan. Spread all but 2 teaspoons of apricot preserves evenly over the chicken pieces. Bake at 425° for about 10 minutes, until the chicken is heated through and well glazed with the preserves.

In a saucepan over high heat bring ½ cup of water to a boil. Add the reserved apricot preserves and carrot slices. Cover and cook for 5 to 6 minutes, until the carrots are tender. Drain the carrots and add them to the couscous along with the green onions and pepper. Toss the mixture well and spoon it onto a serving platter alongside the glazed chicken. Yields 4 servings.

Calories: 473; Fat: 10 g; Cholesterol: 59 mg; Sodium: 79 mg; Carbohydrates: 69 g; Fiber: 0 g; Diabetic Exchange: 2 lower fat meat, 3 starch, 1 fruit, 1 vegetable

CHICKEN BREASTS FLORENTINE

2   *10-ounce packages frozen chopped spinach*
6   *4- to 5-ounce boneless, skinless chicken breasts*
1   *cup water*
1   *stalk celery*
1   *small yellow onion, quartered*
3   *tablespoons flour*
½   *cup skim milk*
¼   *cup Parmesan cheese*
¼   *teaspoon nutmeg*
    Paprika for garnish

Assemble all ingredients and utensils. Preheat the oven to 375°. Cook the spinach according to the package directions. Drain well. In a large saucepan simmer the chicken breasts in water with the celery and onion for 15 minutes. Remove the chicken, reserving 1 cup of the chicken broth. In a saucepan mix the flour with the milk and gradually add the reserved chicken broth. Cook, stirring constantly, until thickened. Stir in the cheese and nutmeg. Add the drained spinach. Spread half the sauce in a 2-quart casserole dish. Layer the chicken over the spinach sauce. Top with the remaining sauce. Sprinkle with paprika. Bake, uncovered, at 375° for 25 to 30 minutes. Serve warm. Yields 6 servings of 8 ounces each.

Calories: 193; Fat: 3 g; Cholesterol: 71 mg; Sodium: 220 mg;
Carbohydrates: 9 g; Fiber: 2 g; Diabetic Exchange: 4 lower fat meat, 1 vegetable

MISS DAISY'S BRUNSWICK STEW

1   *6-pound stewing hen, cut up*
2½ *quarts water*
2   *bay leaves*
2   *large yellow onions, sliced*
2   *cups sliced okra*
4   *cups chopped fresh tomatoes*
3   *cups frozen lima beans*
3   *medium-size potatoes, peeled and diced*
4   *cups fresh or frozen corn kernels*
1   *teaspoon salt*
1   *teaspoon freshly ground black pepper*

Assemble all ingredients and utensils. In a heavy soup pot or Dutch oven combine the hen, water, and bay leaves and cook over low heat for about 2 hours or until the chicken is very tender. Remove the chicken and set it aside to cool. Add the onions, okra, tomatoes, lima beans, potatoes, and corn to the broth. Simmer, uncovered, for about 45 minutes, stirring frequently.

Skin and debone the cooled chicken and cut it into chunks. Return the chicken to the vegetable mixture and season with salt and pepper. Discard the bay leaf. Serve hot. Yields 8 servings of 1 cup each.

Calories: 343; Fat: 7 g; Cholesterol: 43 mg; Sodium: 342 mg; Carbohydrates: 48 g; Fiber: 3 g; Diabetic Exchange: 2 lower fat meat, 2½ starch, 2 vegetable

CORNISH HENS WITH APPLE STUFFING

2   Cornish game hens
1   small yellow onion, chopped
1   apple, peeled, cored, and chopped
1   rib celery, chopped
4   slices whole wheat bread, cubed
2   teaspoons margarine, melted
½   teaspoon dried leaf sage
½   teaspoon dried leaf thyme
¼   teaspoon ground black pepper

Assemble all ingredients and utensils. Preheat the oven to 375°. Rinse the hens and open each cavity for the stuffing. In a medium bowl combine the remaining ingredients. Fill the hen cavities with the stuffing. Place the hens breast-side up in a shallow baking pan. Roast at 375° for 40 to 50 minutes or until the hens are tender. Remove the hens from the pan and slice each in half. Yields 4 servings.

Calories: 265; Fat: 12 g; Cholesterol: 60 mg; Sodium: 222 mg;
Carbohydrates: 18.3 g; Fiber: 2.9 g; Diabetic Exchange: 3 lower fat meat, 1 starch

MY FAVORITE CHICKEN SALAD

Serve as a salad or as a sandwich with low-calorie whole wheat bread.

2   cups cooked chicken breast, chopped
¾   cup sliced celery
¼   cup chopped green onions
½   cup plain low-fat yogurt
1   tablespoon reduced-calorie mayonnaise
1   tablespoon slivered almonds, toasted
1½   teaspoons minced fresh basil or tarragon
½   teaspoon freshly ground black pepper

Assemble all ingredients and utensils. In a large bowl combine the chicken, celery, onions, yogurt, mayonnaise, almonds, basil, and pepper. Toss lightly. Immediately serve or refrigerate. Yields 3 cups or 6 servings of ½ cup each.

Calories: 104; Fat: 4 g; Cholesterol: 37 mg; Sodium: 70 mg; Carbohydrates: 3 g; Fiber: 0.1 g; Diabetic Exchange: 2 lower fat meat

OPEN-FACE CHICKEN SANDWICH

2   *3-ounce boneless chicken breasts, cut into strips*
¼   *cup finely grated Cheddar cheese*
1   *tablespoon plain nonfat yogurt*
1   *tablespoon Dijon mustard*
1   *teaspoon fresh-squeezed lemon juice*
    Lettuce leaves
6   *asparagus spears, cooked and drained*
2   *slices sourdough bread*

Assemble all ingredients and utensils. Either grill the chicken breast strips or microwave them on high for 6 to 8 minutes.

In a small bowl combine the Cheddar cheese, yogurt, mustard, and lemon juice.

Arrange lettuce leaves on both slices of bread. Layer the chicken and asparagus on top in an alternating pattern. Spread the cheese mixture over the sandwich. Broil the sandwiches for about 5 minutes. Note: Canned asparagus spears may be used; just rinse and drain it. Yields 2 open face sandwiches.

Calories: 284; Fat: 7 g; Cholesterol: 67 mg; Sodium: 550 mg; Carbohydrates: 22 g; Fiber: 0.6 g; Diabetic Exchange: 1½ starch, 3½ lower fat meat, ½ vegetable

TURKEY CUTLETS WITH RED PEPPER SAUCE

1   10-ounce package frozen cauliflower, peas, and baby carrots with Parmesan
      sauce
1   pound turkey breast cutlets, cut ¼-inch thick
¼   teaspoon ground black pepper
2   teaspoons olive oil
1   12-ounce jar roasted red pepper, undrained
¼   cup water
2   tablespoons chopped fresh parsley

Assemble all ingredients and utensils. Prepare the frozen vegetables
according to the package directions. Meanwhile, sprinkle the turkey cutlets with pepper. In a large skillet heat the oil over medium heat. Add the
cutlets and cook for 4 to 6 minutes until cooked through, turning once.
Remove the cutlets to a platter and keep them warm. In a blender or food
processor process the roasted red peppers with their liquid until smooth.
Add the mixture to the drippings in the skillet and stir in the water. Cook
for 3 to 4 minutes, stirring frequently until hot. Toss the vegetables with
the chopped parsley and spoon them onto the platter with the turkey.
Yields 4 servings.

Calories: 241; Fat: 7 g; Cholesterol: 80 mg; Sodium: 877 mg;
Carbohydrates: 8 g; Fiber: 1 g; Diabetic Exchange: 4 lower fat meat, 2 vegetable

TURKEY LOAF WITH DILL SAUCE

2   pounds freshly ground raw turkey
2   cups dry breadcrumbs
½   cup shredded carrot
2   large egg whites
¼   cup finely chopped onion
1   tablespoon chopped parsley
1   teaspoon dry mustard
½   teaspoon ground black pepper
½   cup nonfat mayonnaise
⅓   cup nonfat sour cream
3   tablespoons water
2   tablespoons lemon juice
2   tablespoons Dijon mustard
1   teaspoon dried whole dill

Assemble all ingredients and utensils. Preheat the oven to 350°. In a large bowl combine the turkey, breadcrumbs, carrot, egg whites, onion, parsley, dry mustard, and pepper, and stir well. Place the mixture in an 8 x 4-inch loaf pan and shape the top as a loaf. Bake at 350° for 1 hour and 15 minutes or until the meat is no longer pink. Let the loaf stand for 10 minutes.

In a saucepan combine the remaining ingredients and stir well. Cook over low heat until thoroughly heated, stirring constantly.

Transfer the loaf to a platter and serve with dill sauce. Yields 10 servings.

Calories: 245; Fat: 10 g; Cholesterol: 81 mg; Sodium: 448 mg;
Carbohydrates: 19 g; Fiber: 0.1 g; Diabetic Exchange: 2 meat,
1 starch, 1 vegetable

TURKEY AND ARTICHOKE QUICHE

1   *cup diced cooked turkey breast*
1   *14-ounce can artichoke hearts, quartered*
2   *cups grated part skim mozzarella cheese*
1   *cup evaporated skim milk*
1   *tablespoon minced fresh dill*
2   *tablespoons minced fresh parsley*
2   *eggs*
3   *egg whites, lightly beaten*

Assemble all ingredients and utensils. Preheat the oven to 350°. Spray a quiche pan or 9-inch square baking dish with nonstick cooking spray. Place the turkey and artichokes in the prepared pan. Top with mozzarella cheese. Combine the milk, herbs, and eggs and pour the mixture over the turkey and artichokes. Bake at 350° for 35 to 40 minutes or until firm in the center and lightly browned. Yields 8 servings.

Calories: 176; Fat: 7 g; Cholesterol: 98 mg; Sodium: 217 mg;
Carbohydrates: 11 g; Fiber: 0.5 g; Diabetic Exchange: 1 lower fat meat, 1 milk

TURKEY AND HAM TETRAZZINI

¼   *pound mushrooms, sliced*
1   *10¾-ounce can low-fat cream of mushroom soup*
1   *5-ounce can evaporated skim milk*
1   *teaspoon dried leaf thyme*
½   *teaspoon dried leaf basil*
¼   *teaspoon nutmeg*
2   *tablespoons sherry*
1   *cup cooked very low-fat turkey, cubed*
¼   *cup cooked very low-fat ham, cubed*

2 tablespoons drained, chopped pimientos
5 black olives, sliced
6 ounces spaghetti, broken into 2-inch pieces and cooked
2 tablespoons grated Parmesan cheese

Assemble all ingredients and utensils. Preheat the oven to 350°. In a medium nonstick skillet sauté the mushrooms for 3 to 4 minutes. In a medium bowl mix the soup, milk, thyme, basil, nutmeg, and sherry. Stir in the turkey, ham, pimientos, olives, cooked spaghetti, and mushrooms. Place the mixture in a 2-quart baking dish. Top with the Parmesan. Bake at 350° until hot and browned, about 25 to 30 minutes. Yields 6 servings of ½ cup each.

Calories: 250; Fat: 5 g; Cholesterol: 25 mg; Sodium: 476 mg; Carbohydrates: 32 g; Fiber: 0 g; Diabetic Exchange: 2 lower fat meat, 2 starch

TURKEY POCKETS

1½ cups cubed cooked turkey breast
½ cup coarsely chopped tomato
¾ cup diced celery
2½ tablespoons plain nonfat yogurt
2 tablespoons commercial oil-free Italian dressing
2 6-inch whole wheat pita bread rounds, cut in half crosswise
Green leaf lettuce

Assemble all ingredients and utensils. In a bowl combine the turkey, tomatoe, celery, yogurt, and dressing, and chill.

Line the pita halves with leaf lettuce. Spoon ½ cup of the turkey mixture into each half. Yields 4 servings of ½ pita sandwich each.

Calories: 138; Fat: 2 g; Cholesterol: 14 mg; Sodium: 707 mg; Carbohydrates: 20 g; Fiber: 0.9 g; Diabetic Exchange: 1 lower fat meat, 1 starch, 1 vegetable

SEAFOOD QUICHE

2   *eggs or equivalent egg substitute, beaten*
4   *egg whites, beaten well*
6   *ounces precooked shrimp, peeled and deveined*
6   *ounces cooked flaked crab meat*
2   *chopped green onions*
½   *cup thinly sliced fresh mushrooms*
1¼ *cups evaporated skim milk*
2   *cups grated low-fat Swiss cheese*

Assemble all ingredients and utensils. Preheat the oven to 350°. Spray a 9-inch pie pan or quiche pan with nonstick cooking spray. In a large bowl combine all of the ingredients and pour the mixture into the prepared pan. Bake at 350° for 35 to 45 minutes, until firm and lightly browned. Yields 8 servings.

Calories: 178; Fat: 5 g; Cholesterol: 68 mg; Sodium: 271 mg; Carbohydrates: 5 g; Fiber: 0.1 g; Diabetic Exchange: 3 lower fat meat, ½ skim milk

SAUTÉED SEA SCALLOPS

1   *pound sea scallops, sliced horizontally*
6   *fresh mushrooms, sliced*
½   *green bell pepper, diced*
1   *medium tomato, chopped*
¼   *cup dry white wine*
2   *green onions, chopped*
½   *teaspoon dried dill*

Assemble all ingredients and utensils. Rinse the scallops and pat dry. In a large nonstick skillet combine the mushrooms, bell pepper, tomato, and wine and cook for about 5 minutes, until the vegetables are tender. Add the onions, scallops, and dill, and cook for about 5 to 7 minutes, until the scallops are clear. Yields 4 servings of approximately 4 ounces each.

Calories: 125; Fat: 1 g; Cholesterol: 37 mg; Sodium: 186 mg; Carbohydrates: 6 g; Fiber: 0.4 g; Diabetic Exchange: 3 lower fat meat, 1 vegetable

MISS DAISY'S SHRIMP CREOLE

Serve over rice.

½   *medium yellow onion, chopped*
2   *cloves garlic, minced*
4   *ounces sliced fresh mushrooms*
½   *cup chopped celery*
½   *cup chopped green bell pepper*
½   *cup dry white wine*
1   *8-ounce can low-sodium tomato sauce*
¼   *teaspoon hot sauce*
3   *bay leaves*
1   *pound medium shrimp, peeled and deveined*

Assemble all ingredients and utensils. In a large skillet sauté the onion, garlic, mushrooms, celery, and pepper in the white wine for 4 to 5 minutes. Add the tomato sauce, hot sauce, and bay leaves. Cover and bring the mixture to a boil, then simmer for 10 minutes. Add the shrimp and cook, uncovered, for 5 to 10 minutes, until the shrimp is done. Remove the bay leaves before serving. Tastes great when reheated. Yields 8 servings of 4 ounces each.

Calories: 60; Fat: 1 g; Cholesterol: 43 mg; Sodium: 235 mg; Carbohydrates: 5 g; Fiber: 0.2 g; Diabetic Exchange: 2 vegetable, 2 lower fat meat

SHRIMP SCAMPI

2   teaspoons olive oil
8   cloves garlic, finely chopped
2   pounds peeled and deveined shrimp
1   tablespoon seeded, minced red chile pepper
1   tablespoon lime juice

Assemble all ingredients and utensils. Spray a large skillet with nonstick cooking spray. Add the oil and garlic and cook over medium high heat for 1 minute. Add the shrimp and pepper and cook for 5 minutes, stirring constantly. Add the lime juice and cook an additional 3 to 4 minutes or until the shrimp turns pink. Yields 4 servings.

Calories: 149; Fat: 4 g; Cholesterol: 170 mg; Sodium: 168 mg;
Carbohydrates: 4 g; Fiber: 0 g; Diabetic Exchange: 3 lower fat meat

CRAB CAKES

½   cup crushed saltine crackers
1   cup cooked, flaked crab meat
1   stalk celery, chopped
1   tablespoon finely chopped onion
2   egg whites
2   teaspoons margarine
    Tabasco sauce

Assemble all ingredients and utensils. In a medium bowl combine all of the ingredients except the margarine and Tabasco, and mix until well blended. Shape into 4 patties. Melt the margarine in a large skillet and brown the patties, turning once. Cook for approximately 5 to 7 minutes on each side. Serve warm. Top each patty with a splash of Tabasco sauce. Yields 4 patties.

Calories: 121; Fat: 4 g; Cholesterol: 30 mg; Sodium: 760 mg; Carbohydrates: 7 g; Fiber: 0.1 g; Diabetic Exchange: 2 lower fat meat, ½ starch, ½ fat

SALMON LOAF

1   7½-ounce can salmon, drained, boned, and flaked
2   cups soft whole wheat breadcrumbs
4   egg whites, beaten
⅓   cup skim milk
½   cup chopped onion
1   tablespoon minced fresh parsley
1   teaspoon minced fresh dill
¼   teaspoon freshly ground black pepper
¼   teaspoon dry mustard
2   tablespoons lemon juice

Assemble all ingredients and utensils. Preheat the oven to 400°. Spray a 4 x 8-inch loaf pan with nonstick cooking spray. In a large bowl combine all of the ingredients. Place the mixture in the prepared loaf pan. Bake at 400° for 25 to 30 minutes. Serve hot with Dill Sauce (see recipe with Turkey Loaf on page 179). Yields 4 8-ounce servings.

Calories: 98; Fat: 3 g; Cholesterol: 20 mg; Sodium: 298 mg; Carbohydrates: 8 g; Fiber: 1 g; Diabetic Exchange: 1 lower fat meat, ½ starch

LEMON DILL SALMON STEAKS

1   *teaspoon safflower oil*
2   *tablespoons fresh lemon juice*
2   *tablespoons minced fresh dill*
4   *6-ounce salmon steaks*

Assemble all ingredients and utensils. In a shallow bowl combine the oil, lemon juice, and dill, and let the mixture stand for 20 minutes. Dip the salmon in the mixture and place it on a broiler rack. Broil for about 7 to 10 minutes. Turn and brush with additional oil. Broil for another 10 minutes or until the fish flakes and is browned. Garnish with fresh dill and lemon slices. Yields 4 servings of 5 ounces each.

Calories: 317; Fat: 19 g; Cholesterol: 111 mg; Sodium: 80 mg; Carbohydrates: 0.9 g; Fiber: 0 g; Diabetic Exchange: 5 lower fat meat

ALMOND DILL BAKED FISH

2   *egg whites, beaten until foamy*
2   *tablespoons skim milk*
¼   *cup wheat germ*
2   *tablespoons ground almonds*
⅓   *cup wheat bran*
⅓   *cup freshly grated Parmesan cheese*
1   *teaspoon fresh chopped dill*
1½ *pounds flounder or whitefish*

Assemble all ingredients and utensils. Preheat the oven to 350°. Spray a baking pan with nonstick cooking spray. In a shallow bowl combine the egg whites and milk. In a separate shallow pan combine the remaining ingredients except the fish. Dip the fish in the milk mixture and then the dry mixture. Place the fish on the prepared pan. Bake at 350° for 8 to 10 minutes or until the fish flakes easily. Broil for 1 minute to brown. Garnish with dill, lemon, and fresh parsley. Yields 6 servings of 4 ounces each.

Calories: 169; Fat: 5 g; Cholesterol: 58 mg; Sodium: 195 mg;
Carbohydrates: 6 g; Fiber: 2 g; Diabetic Exchange: 4 lower fat meat, ½ starch

SALMON PATTIES WITH GREEN PEAS

1	*1-pound can red salmon*
2	*large egg whites*
1	*tablespoon finely chopped onion*
¼	*teaspoon ground black pepper*
¼	*teaspoon dried dill*
1	*cup crushed saltine crackers*
1	*cup fat-free chicken broth*
1	*tablespoon cornstarch*
1	*tablespoon margarine*
1	*cup drained canned green peas*

Assemble all ingredients and utensils. Preheat the oven to 350°. Grease a baking sheet with a small amount of margarine. Drain the salmon and pour the liquid into a mixing bowl. Discard the bones and dark skin from the salmon, and set the rest aside. Add the egg whites, onion, pepper, and dill to the salmon juice and mix together with a fork. Add the cracker crumbs and salmon to the egg white mixture and mix lightly.

Shape into patties about ¾-inch thick using ⅓ cup of mixture per patty. Place the patties on the prepared baking sheet. Bake at 350° for 35 to 40 minutes, until firm and lightly browned. In a saucepan stir the broth and cornstarch together until smooth. Cook until thickened. Add the margarine and peas to the sauce and reheat to serving temperature. Yields 6 servings of 1 patty with ⅓ cup sauce each.

Calories: 214; Fat: 9 g; Cholesterol: 33 g; Sodium: 639 mg; Carbohydrates: 13 g; Fiber: 1 g; Diabetic Exchange: 2 lower fat meat, 1 starch

SHRIMP STIR-FRY

Serve with rice or noodles.

½ *pound shrimp, peeled and deveined*
1   *small yellow onion, sliced*
1   *teaspoon chopped garlic*
1   *cup fresh snow peas*
1   *cup sliced carrots*
1   *cup sliced mushrooms*
1   *cup sliced bell peppers*
3   *tablespoons water*
1   *teaspoon soy sauce*

Assemble all ingredients and utensils. Spray a large skillet with nonstick cooking spray. Add the shrimp, onion, and garlic, and stir-fry until the shrimp is cooked, about 8 to 10 minutes. Remove the shrimp and keep it warm. Stir-fry the remaining vegetables, adding water as needed to prevent sticking. Add the soy sauce just before serving. Yields 4 servings.

Calories: 77; Fat: 0.8 g; Cholesterol: 43 mg; Sodium: 140 mg;
Carbohydrates: 10 g; Fiber: 2 g; Diabetic Exchange: 1 lower fat meat, 2 vegetable

OPEN-FACE TUNA SANDWICH

¼   cup reduced-calorie mayonnaise
½   teaspoon curry powder
1   6½-ounce can water-packed tuna, drained
¾   cup chopped red apple with peel
1   tablespoon raisins
½   cup finely chopped celery
1   tablespoon minced green onion or chives
4   slices raisin or low-calorie whole wheat bread

Assemble all ingredients and utensils. In a large bowl mix together the mayonnaise and curry powder. Stir in the tuna, apple, raisins, celery, and onion or chives until blended. Toast the bread and spread equal portions of tuna mixture over each slice. Yields 4 open-faced sandwiches.

Calories: 167; Fat: 5 g; Cholesterol: 13 mg; Sodium: 382 mg;
Carbohydrates: 14 g; Fiber: 3 g; Diabetic Exchange: 2 lower fat meat,
1 starch, 1 fat

CRAB MEAT SALAD ON TOASTED ENGLISH MUFFINS

½   medium red bell pepper, finely chopped
¼   cup finely chopped celery
2   tablespoons chopped green onions
1½ tablespoons nonfat mayonnaise
1½ teaspoons Dijon mustard
½   teaspoon lemon juice
1   6½-ounce can white crab meat, drained
2   English muffins, split and toasted
4   tomato slices, ¼-inch thick
¼   cup shredded reduced-fat sharp Cheddar cheese
    Freshly ground black pepper

Assemble all ingredients and utensils. In a medium bowl combine the red pepper, celery, onions, mayonnaise, mustard, and lemon juice. Stir in the crab meat. Toast the English muffin halves. Spoon the crab meat mixture evenly over the muffin halves. Top each serving with a tomato slice. Sprinkle evenly with the Cheddar cheese and black pepper. Broil for 3 to 4 minutes or until the cheese melts. Yields 4 servings.

Calories: 152; Fat: 2 g; Cholesterol: 46 mg; Sodium: 495 mg;
Carbohydrates: 17 g; Fiber: 0.4 g; Diabetic Exchange: 1½ lower fat meat, 1 starch

HOT TOMATO SANDWICH

¼   *cup low-fat ricotta cheese*
1   *slice whole wheat toast*
2   *tomato slices, ⅛-inch thick*
½   *teaspoon Dijon mustard*
¼   *teaspoon chopped fresh basil*

Assemble all ingredients and utensils. Spread the ricotta cheese on the wheat toast. Top with the tomato slices. Spread the mustard and fresh basil over the tomato. Broil until the tomato is hot. Yields 1 sandwich.

Calories: 159; Fat: 6 g; Cholesterol: 20 mg; Sodium: 277 mg;
Carbohydrates: 17 g; Fiber: 2 g; Diabetic Exchange: 1 lower fat meat, 1 starch

MEXICAN QUICHE

½   cup chopped yellow onion
¾   cup chopped red bell pepper
½   cup chopped green bell pepper
¼   cup water
10 ounces shredded Monterey Jack cheese
2   eggs
4   egg whites, beaten until foamy
1¼ cups skim milk
1   teaspoon dried leaf basil
⅛   teaspoon ground black pepper
⅛   teaspoon paprika

Assemble all ingredients and utensils. Spray a quiche pan or 8-inch pie pan with nonstick cooking spray. Sauté the onion and bell peppers in water until tender. Drain and transfer the mixture to the quiche pan. Sprinkle with Monterey Jack cheese. In a small bowl combine the eggs, egg whites, milk, and spices. Pour the mixture over the cheese. Bake at 350° for 40 to 45 minutes or until firm in the center. Yields 8 servings.

Calories: 180; Fat: 12 g; Cholesterol: 100 mg; Sodium: 251 mg;
Carbohydrates: 4 g; Fiber: 0.3 g; Diabetic Exchange: 2 high fat meat

BASIL TOMATO QUICHE

2   large tomatoes, peeled, seeded, and chopped
4   egg whites
8   basil leaves, torn into small pieces
⅛   teaspoon garlic powder
1   cup evaporated skim milk
2   tablespoons grated Parmesan cheese
1   cup grated low-fat mozzarella cheese

Assemble all ingredients and utensils. Preheat the oven to 350°. Spray an 8-inch pie pan or quiche pan with nonstick cooking spray. Drain any juice from the tomatoes. In a medium bowl beat the egg whites until frothy. In a large bowl combine the remaining ingredients. Stir in the tomatoes and fold in the egg whites. Pour the mixture into the pan. Bake at 350° for 35 to 40 minutes, until browned. Yields 8 servings.

Calories: 82; Fat: 3 g; Cholesterol: 10 mg; Sodium: 161 mg; Carbohydrates: 5 g; Fiber: 0.2 g; Diabetic Exchange: 1 lower fat meat, 1 vegetable

RED BEANS AND RICE

2   *cloves garlic, minced*
1/3 *cup diced onion*
1/8 *teaspoon each, cayenne pepper, cumin, and chili powder*
2   *teaspoons Tabasco sauce*
2   *cups cooked brown rice*
2   *cups cooked red beans*
1/2 *cup diced cooked low-fat ham*

Assemble all ingredients and utensils. Spray a saucepan with nonstick cooking spray. Sauté the garlic and onion with the seasonings. Add the rice, beans, and ham, and cook over medium heat. Stir in 1/4 cup water or more if needed. Cook until heated through. Yields 4 servings of 1 cup each.

Calories: 261; Fat: 2 g; Cholesterol: 9 mg; Sodium: 214 mg; Carbohydrates: 47 g; Fiber: 4 g; Diabetic Exchange: 3 starch, 1/2 meat

BLACK BEAN CHILI

4   15-ounce cans black beans, rinsed and drained
3   cups mild salsa
1   11-ounce can corn kernels, drained
1   cup grated pepper jack cheese (about 4 ounces)

Assemble all ingredients and utensils. In a very large saucepan over high heat cook the beans, salsa, and corn for 6 to 7 minutes, stirring frequently until hot. Remove the bean mixture from the heat. Stir in ¾ cup of grated cheese until melted. Serve the chili sprinkled with the remaining ¼ cup of cheese divided equally among the servings. Yields 12 servings of ¾ cup each.

Calories: 223; Fat: 4 g; Cholesterol: 10 mg; Sodium: 734 mg;
Carbohydrates: 30 g; Fiber: 4.8 g; Diabetic Exchange: 1 lower fat meat, 2 starch

PASTA, GRAINS, AND RICE

ANGEL HAIR PASTA WITH ASPARAGUS

2   teaspoons margarine
¼   cup minced green onion
2   small cloves garlic, minced
1   cup frozen asparagus spears, thawed
1   cup nonfat milk
½   cup half and half
2   ounces Parmesan cheese, freshly grated
¼   cup light cream cheese
¼   teaspoon ground white pepper
2   cups cooked angel hair pasta, cooked
     according to package directions without salt

Assemble all ingredients and utensils. In a large skillet heat the margarine
and sauté the green onion and garlic until tender, about 1 minute. Add
the asparagus and cook until crisp and tender. Stir in the remaining
ingredients except the pasta and cook, stirring constantly, until the mixture comes to a boil. Toss the pasta with the sauce and serve immediately.
Yields 4 servings of 1 cup of pasta and ¾ cup of sauce each.

Calories: 284; Fat: 13 g; Cholesterol: 33 mg; Sodium: 389 mg;
Carbohydrates: 27 g; Fiber: 0.3 g; Diabetic Exchange: ½ low-fat milk,
1 lower fat meat, 1 starch, 1 fat, ½ vegetable

FUSILLI WITH SUN-DRIED TOMATOES

8   ounces vegetable-flavored fusilli pasta

1   tablespoon virgin olive oil

½   teaspoon hot pepper flakes

1   large garlic clove, minced

2   green onions, chopped

2   tablespoons sun-dried tomatoes, chopped

1   tablespoon grated orange zest

1   tablespoon tomato paste

½   cup drained and chopped canned Italian plum tomatoes

¼   cup low-fat chicken broth

¼   teaspoon ground black pepper

2   tablespoons fresh chopped chives

1   teaspoon sesame oil

Assemble all ingredients and utensils. In a large pot of boiling water cook the pasta for 8 to 10 minutes. Drain and set the pasta aside. In a large nonstick skillet heat the oil. Add the pepper flakes, garlic, green onions, sun-dried tomatoes, and orange zest. Stir-fry for 1 minute; then add the pasta and stir-fry 1 minute more. Add the tomato paste, plum tomatoes, broth, and pepper. Toss well and cook until heated through. Garnish with chives and drizzle with sesame oil. Yields 6 servings of ¾ cup each.

Calories: 168; Fat: 4 g; Cholesterol: 0 mg; Sodium: 60 mg;
Carbohydrates: 29 g; Fiber: 0.3 g; Diabetic Exchange: 2 starch, 1 fat

PASTA PRIMAVERA

1   tablespoon olive oil
1   cup chopped yellow onion
1   cup diced carrots
1   cup broccoli flowerets
1   cup sliced fresh mushrooms
½   cup chopped zucchini
1   28-ounce can crushed tomatoes, drained
1   clove garlic, minced
1   tablespoon dried leaf basil
¼   teaspoon salt
¼   teaspoon ground black pepper
¼   teaspoon nutmeg
1   cup frozen green peas, thawed
3   cups cooked fettuccine
⅓   cup grated Parmesan cheese

Assemble all ingredients and utensils. In a large saucepan heat the oil and
sauté the onion, carrots, and broccoli. When the onion begins to soften
add the mushrooms and zucchini and sauté for 5 more minutes. Add the
tomatoes, garlic, basil, salt, pepper, and nutmeg. Simmer for 5 minutes.
Add the peas and heat through. Toss with cooked fettuccine and sprinkle
Parmesan cheese over all. Yields 6 servings of 1 cup each.

Calories: 214; Fat: 5 g; Cholesterol: 4 mg; Sodium: 438 mg;
Carbohydrates: 36 g; Fiber: 3 g; Diabetic Exchange: 1½ starch, 2 vegetable, 1 fat

SPINACH LINGUINE

4 garlic cloves, minced
½ cup low-fat chicken broth
1 10-ounce package frozen chopped spinach, cooked
1 teaspoon dried leaf basil
½ teaspoon ground black pepper
12 ounces linguine, cooked and drained
⅓ cup grated Parmesan cheese

Assemble all ingredients and utensils. In a large saucepan over medium heat sauté the garlic for 2 minutes. Add the chicken broth, cooked spinach, basil, and black pepper. Combine the cooked linguine, spinach mixture, and Parmesan until mixed. Serve immediately. Yields 6 servings of 1 cup each.

Calories: 246; Fat: 2 g; Cholesterol: 4 mg; Sodium: 117 mg; Carbohydrates: 46 g; Fiber: 0.8 g; Diabetic Exchange: 3 starch

COUSCOUS WITH MUSHROOMS AND GREEN ONIONS

1 tablespoon safflower oil
4 cups thinly sliced fresh mushrooms
1 teaspoon minced fresh garlic
1¼ cups low-fat chicken broth
½ teaspoon dried leaf oregano
⅛ teaspoon freshly ground black pepper
1 cup couscous
¼ cup minced green onion

Assemble all ingredients and utensils. In a medium saucepan heat the oil and sauté the mushrooms and garlic for about 8 minutes. Add the broth and seasonings and bring the mixture to a boil. Stir in the dry couscous and green onion. Cover and remove the pan from the heat, allowing the pasta to stand for 5 minutes. Stir the mixture again and serve immediately. Yields 6 servings of ½ cup each.

Calories: 132; Fat: 3 g; Cholesterol: 0 mg; Sodium: 6 mg; Carbohydrates: 23 g; Fiber: 2 g; Diabetic Exchange: 1 vegetable, 1 starch, 1 fat

PARMESAN FETTUCCINE

3   *tablespoons low-calorie margarine*
1   *cup evaporated skim milk*
10 *ounces whole wheat fettuccine, cooked and drained*
½   *cup grated Parmesan cheese*
½   *teaspoon freshly ground black pepper*
¼   *teaspoon nutmeg*

Assemble all ingredients and utensils. In a small saucepan melt the margarine. Add the evaporated milk and heat until hot, but do not boil. Quickly toss in the fettuccine and Parmesan. Stir in the black pepper and nutmeg. Serve immediately. Yields 6 servings of ¾ cup each.

Calories: 248; Fat: 6 g; Cholesterol: 7 mg; Sodium: 206 mg; Carbohydrates: 34 g; Fiber: 5 g; Diabetic Exchange: 2 starch, ½ low-fat milk, ½ fat

CORN AND TOMATO POLENTA

4   cups water
¼   teaspoon salt
1   cup yellow cornmeal or polenta
½   cup tomato sauce
1   teaspoon dried leaf oregano
¾   cup whole-kernel corn, drained
¼   teaspoon crushed hot pepper flakes
¼   teaspoon ground black pepper

Assemble all ingredients and utensils. In a large saucepan bring the water and salt to a boil. Slowly pour the cornmeal into the saucepan, so that the water does not stop boiling. When the water is absorbed, reduce the heat and simmer for 20 to 25 minutes. Meanwhile, in a separate saucepan heat the tomato sauce, oregano, corn, hot pepper flakes, and black pepper. Layer half of the cornmeal mixture in an 8 x 8-inch pan or 1½-quart casserole dish and top with half of the sauce. Top with the remaining cornmeal and sauce. Cut in squares and serve immediately. Yields 6 servings of 4 ounces each.

Calories: 105; Fat: 0 g; Cholesterol: 0 mg; Sodium: 283 mg;
Carbohydrates: 24 g; Fiber: 0.1 g; Diabetic Exchange: 1½ bread/starch

MUSHROOM BARLEY CASSEROLE

¼   cup water
1   cup chopped onion
½   pound fresh mushrooms, sliced
1   cup barley
2   cups low-sodium beef or chicken stock
¼   teaspoon ground black pepper
¼   teaspoon ground marjoram

Assemble all ingredients and utensils. In a saucepan sauté the onion and mushrooms in water until tender. Stir in the barley and brown lightly. Add the stock and seasonings, and mix well. Cover tightly and simmer over low heat for 1 hour, until the barley is tender and the liquid absorbed. Yields 4 servings.

Calories: 203; Fat: 0.8 g; Cholesterol: 0 mg; Sodium: 7 mg;
Carbohydrates: 45 g; Fiber: 1 g; Diabetic Exchange: 2½ starch, 1 vegetable

ORZO WITH PINE NUTS

8   ounces orzo
1   tablespoon virgin olive oil
¼   cup pine nuts
1   tablespoon dried leaf basil
¼   teaspoon salt
¼   teaspoon freshly ground black pepper

Assemble all ingredients and utensils. In a large pot of boiling water cook the orzo until al dente, about 3 minutes. Drain. In a nonstick skillet heat the oil and stir in the pine nuts. Cook for 5 minutes. Add the orzo, basil, salt, and pepper. Heat through and serve immediately. Yields 6 servings of ½ cup each.

Calories: 196; Fat: 6 g; Cholesterol: 0 mg; Sodium: 96 mg;
Carbohydrates: 29 g; Fiber: 0 g; Diabetic Exchange: 2 starch, 1 fat

MISS DAISY'S GARLIC CHEESE GRITS

2¼ cups water
¼   teaspoon salt
¾   cup quick-cooking grits, uncooked
½   cup shredded reduced-fat sharp Cheddar cheese
2   cloves garlic, crushed
¼   teaspoon hot sauce
¼   cup frozen egg substitute, thawed

Assemble all ingredients and utensils. Preheat the oven to 350°. Spray a 1-quart baking dish with nonstick cooking spray. In a medium saucepan combine the water and salt and bring it to a boil. Stir in the grits. Cover, reduce the heat, and simmer for 5 minutes or until the mixture is thickened, stirring occasionally. Remove the pan from the heat.

Add the cheese, garlic, and hot sauce, stirring until the cheese melts. Gradually stir about one fourth of the hot grits mixture into the egg substitute. Add the egg substitute mixture to the remaining grits mixture, stirring constantly.

Spoon the grits into the prepared dish. Bake at 350° for 30 minutes or until set. Garnish with fresh parsley. Yields 6 servings of ½ cup each.

Calories: 104; Fat: 2 g; Cholesterol: 7 mg; Sodium: 184 mg;
Carbohydrates: 15 g; Fiber: 0 g; Diabetic Exchange: 1 starch, ½ lower fat meat

CHEESY RICE CASSEROLE

2½ cups cooked brown rice
3   green onions, chopped
1   cup low-fat cottage cheese
1   teaspoon dried dill
¼   cup freshly grated Parmesan cheese

½   cup low-fat milk

1   teaspoon Dijon mustard

Assemble all ingredients and utensils. Preheat the oven to 350°. Spray a 2-quart casserole dish with nonstick cooking spray. In a large bowl combine all of the ingredients, mixing well. Pour the mixture into the prepared dish. Bake at 350° for 30 to 35 minutes. Yields 6 servings of ¾ cup each.

Calories: 152; Fat: 2 g; Cholesterol: 4 mg; Sodium: 248 mg;
Carbohydrates: 23 g; Fiber: 0.3 g; Diabetic Exchange: 1 starch, ½ lower fat meat

PILAF OF BROWN RICE

½   cup diced carrot

½   cup diced red bell pepper

¼   cup sliced fresh mushrooms

1   cup brown rice, uncooked

2   large cloves garlic, minced

¼   teaspoon salt

½   teaspoon dried leaf oregano

½   teaspoon dried leaf thyme

3   cups water

Assemble all ingredients and utensils. In a saucepan steam or blanch the carrot, pepper, and mushrooms until tender but crisp. Drain well and set them aside. In a large saucepan combine the rice and remaining ingredients. Bring the mixture to a boil. Cover, reduce the heat, and simmer for 45 minutes.

Add the vegetable mixture to the rice mixture and toss. Cover and cook an additional 5 to 8 minutes or until the rice is cooked and the liquid is absorbed. Yields 8 servings of ½ cup each.

Calories: 49; Fat: 0.5 g; Cholesterol: 0 mg; Sodium: 75 mg;
Carbohydrates: 10 g; Fiber: 0.7 g; Diabetic Exchange: ½ starch

SUN-DRIED TOMATO AND BLACK BEAN PILAF

1   *tablespoon olive oil*
1   *medium onion, chopped*
1   *cup sliced mushrooms*
1¾ *cups low-fat chicken broth*
1½ *cups sun-dried tomatoes, chopped*
¾   *cup instant brown rice*
1   *15-ounce can black beans, rinsed and drained*
2   *teaspoons dried leaf basil*
½   *teaspoon ground black pepper*

Assemble all ingredients and utensils. In a medium saucepan heat the oil over medium heat. Add the onion and mushrooms and cook for 3 minutes, stirring occasionally. Add the broth and tomatoes and bring the mixture to a boil. Stir in the rice and beans and return the mixture to a boil. Reduce the heat to low, cover, and simmer for 12 minutes or until all of the broth is absorbed. Stir in the basil and black pepper. Serve hot. Yields 6 servings of ½ cup each.

Calories: 190; Fat: 3 g; Cholesterol: 0 mg; Sodium: 25 mg; Carbohydrates: 34 g; Fiber: 5 g; Diabetic Exchange: 2 vegetable, 1½ starch, ½ fat

OATMEAL WITH APPLESAUCE

2 *cups skim milk*
1 *cup regular oats, uncooked*
1 *cup unsweetened cinnamon applesauce*
1 *tablespoon brown sugar*
¼ *teaspoon vanilla extract*

Assemble all ingredients and utensils. Heat the milk in a heavy saucepan until hot, but not boiling. Stir in the oats and cook for 5 minutes or until thickened, stirring occasionally. Add the applesauce and remaining ingredients and cook for 1 minute, stirring frequently, until heated. Yields 4 servings of ¾ cup each.

Calories: 152; Fat: 2 g; Cholesterol: 2 mg; Sodium: 65 mg;
Carbohydrates: 28 g; Fiber: 3 g; Diabetic Exchange: ½ milk, ½ fruit, 1 starch

13

VEGETABLES AND SIDE DISHES

CHILLED ASPARAGUS

1½ *pounds fresh asparagus, trimmed*
⅓   *cup strawberry vinegar*
2   *teaspoons walnut oil*
¼   *cup water*
2   *teaspoons honey*

Assemble all ingredients and utensils. Steam the asparagus until crisp but tender. Immediately drop it into ice water. Drain. Cut each stalk into thirds. In a large bowl combine the vinegar, oil, water, and honey. Toss the asparagus with the dressing. Chill well before serving. Yields 4 servings of ¾ cup each.

Calories: 55; Fat: 3 g; Cholesterol: 0 g; Sodium: 3 mg;
Carbohydrates: 8 g; Fiber: 1 g; Diabetic Exchange: 1 vegetable, ½ fat

LEMON GINGER BROCCOLI

1   *bunch broccoli (1¼ to 1½ pounds)*
1   *tablespoon vegetable oil*
2   *teaspoons minced ginger root*
1   *tablespoon freshly squeezed lemon juice*
    Freshly ground black pepper

Assemble all ingredients and utensils. Cut the broccoli into ½-inch thick pieces. Steam for 3 to 5 minutes or until tender; or boil in a saucepan until crisp but tender, about 10 minutes. Drain the broccoli and it set aside. In a skillet heat the oil over medium heat. Add the ginger root and cook for 2 minutes. Stir in the lemon juice. Pour the lemon juice mixture over the broccoli and sprinkle with black pepper. Reheat before serving. Yields 6 servings of ½ cup each.

Calories: 34; Fat: 2 g; Cholesterol: 0 mg; Sodium: 12 mg;
Carbohydrates: 3 g; Fiber: 0.6 g; Diabetic Exchange: ½ vegetable, ½ fat

ORIENTAL CAULIFLOWER

4½ *cups chopped cauliflower*
1   *teaspoon toasted sesame seeds*
1   *teaspoon soy sauce*
2   *tablespoons lemon juice*
2   *tablespoons pineapple juice concentrate*
½   *teaspoon sesame oil*

Assemble all ingredients and utensils. Steam the cauliflower for about 3 to 4 minutes or boil in a saucepan until tender, about 15 to 20 minutes.

Drain. In a medium bowl combine the remaining ingredients and stir in the cauliflower. Serve hot or cold. Yields 4 servings of 1 cup each.

Calories: 54; Fat: 1 g; Cholesterol: 0 mg; Sodium: 102 mg; Carbohydrates: 10 g; Fiber: 1 g; Diabetic Exchange: 2 vegetable

GINGERED CARROTS

4   cups julienned carrots
2   teaspoons reduced-calorie margarine
2   teaspoons brown sugar
¼   teaspoon ground ginger

Assemble all ingredients and utensils. Steam the carrots until tender but crisp, about 3 to 5 minutes, or boil in a saucepan for about 10 to 15 minutes. Drain. Meanwhile, in a medium saucepan melt the margarine . Stir in the brown sugar and ginger. Cook over medium heat until the sugar dissolves. Stir frequently. Add the drained carrots and continue cooking, stirring gently, for 2 minutes. Yields 4 servings of 1 cup each.

Calories: 64; Fat: 1 g; Cholesterol: 0 g; Sodium: 48 mg; Carbohydrates: 13 g; Fiber: 2 g; Diabetic Exchange: 2 vegetable

SOUTHERN-STYLE GREEN BEANS

1   *pound fresh green beans*
1   *cup canned low-sodium beef or chicken broth*
1   *small yellow onion, quartered*
⅓   *cup chopped lean, low-fat cooked ham*
1   *bay leaf*
½   *teaspoon salt*
¼   *teaspoon freshly ground black pepper*

Assemble all ingredients and utensils. String the green beans and cut them into 1½-inch pieces. Wash the beans thoroughly and drain. In a large saucepan combine the beans and remaining ingredients. Bring the broth to a boil. Cover the pan and reduce the heat. Cook over low heat for 45 to 50 minutes or until the beans are tender. Stir occasionally. Discard the bay leaf before serving. Yields 6 servings of ½ cup each.

Calories: 32; Fat: 0.5 g; Cholesterol: 4 mg; Sodium: 293 mg; Carbohydrates: 5 g; Fiber: 1 g; Diabetic Exchange: 1 vegetable

CORN CASSEROLE

1   *17-ounce can whole-kernel corn*
1   *small red bell pepper, chopped*
1   *medium green bell pepper, chopped*
    Egg substitute equivalent to 2 eggs
½   *cup low-fat milk*
2   *tablespoons all-purpose flour*
1   *packet sugar substitute*
2   *tablespoons reduced-calorie margarine*

Assemble all ingredients and utensils. Preheat the oven to 350°. Spray a 1½-quart casserole dish with nonstick cooking spray. In a large bowl combine all of the ingredients. Mix well. Pour the mixture into the prepared dish. Bake at 350° for 45 to 50 minutes. Yields 6 servings of ½ cup each.

Calories: 109; Fat: 4 g; Cholesterol: 0.2 mg; Sodium: 269 mg; Carbohydrates: 16 g; Fiber: 1 g; Diabetic Exchange: 1 starch, ½ fat

CREOLE CABBAGE

5   cups chopped cabbage
2   tablespoons reduced-calorie margarine
1   large onion, chopped
1   green bell pepper, chopped
1   16-ounce can tomatoes, diced
1   packet sugar substitute
½   teaspoon ground black pepper
¼   teaspoon salt
½   cup low-fat grated Cheddar cheese

Assemble all ingredients and utensils. Preheat the oven to 325°. In a large pot cook the cabbage in boiling salted water for 10 minutes. Drain well and place the cabbage in a baking pan. In a large skillet melt the margarine and sauté the onion and green pepper. Add the tomatoes with juice, sugar substitute, pepper, and salt, and simmer for 5 to 10 minutes. Pour the mixture over the cabbage. Sprinkle with Cheddar cheese. Bake at 325° for about 20 minutes or until the cheese melts. Yields 8 servings of ½ cup each.

Calories: 65; Fat: 3 g; Cholesterol: 5 mg; Sodium: 241 mg; Carbohydrates: 7 g; Fiber: 1 g; Diabetic Exchange: 1½ vegetable, ½ fat

OVEN–FRIED OKRA

1   *pound fresh okra*
¾   *cup yellow cornmeal*
¼   *teaspoon salt*
⅛   *teaspoon ground black pepper*
¼   *cup nonfat buttermilk*
1   *egg, lightly beaten*

Assemble all ingredients and utensils. Preheat the oven to 450°. Wash the okra and snip the top and bottom from each pod. Cut the okra into ½-inch pieces. In a shallow bowl combine the cornmeal, salt, and pepper.

In a large bowl combine the buttermilk and egg. Stir in the okra and let it stand for a few minutes. Coat the okra with the cornmeal mixture. Place the okra on a nonstick baking pan. Bake at 450° for 40 to 45 minutes or until crisp. Yields 6 servings of ½ cup each.

Calories: 99; Fat: 1 g; Cholesterol: 46 mg; Sodium: 115 mg;
Carbohydrates: 18 g; Fiber: 0.8 g; Diabetic Exchange: 1 vegetable, 1 starch

ROASTED ONIONS

4   *large onions, peeled and cut in half lengthwise*
½   *teaspoon leaf savory*
1   *tablespoon balsamic vinegar*
1   *tablespoon minced fresh parsley*

Assemble all ingredients and utensils. Preheat the oven to 350°. In a baking dish mist the onions with nonstick olive oil spray. Sprinkle with the savory. Bake at 350° for 45 to 50 minutes, until tender. Remove the onions from the oven and sprinkle with the vinegar and parsley. Yields 4 servings of 2 halves each.

Calories: 28; Fat: 0.2 g; Cholesterol: 0 mg; Sodium: 2 mg;
Carbohydrates: 6 g; Fiber: 0.6 g; Diabetic Exchange: 1 vegetable

DILL NEW POTATOES

1   *pound new potatoes with skin on, washed*
1   *tablespoon reduced-calorie margarine*
1   *tablespoon freshly chopped dill*
1   *teaspoon freshly ground black pepper*

Assemble all ingredients and utensils. In a large pot cook the potatoes in boiling water until tender; about 25 to 30 minutes. Drain. Quarter the potatoes and toss them in a bowl with the margarine, dill, and black pepper. Yields 4 servings of ½ cup each.

Calories: 75; Fat: 2 g; Cholesterol: 0 mg; Sodium: 19 mg;
Carbohydrates: 14 g; Fiber: 0.4 g; Diabetic Exchange: 1 starch, ½ fat

MISS DAISY'S CHIVE MASHED POTATOES

4   *cups peeled, cubed baking potatoes*
½   *cup skim milk*
½   *cup plain nonfat yogurt*
1   *clove garlic, minced*
½   *teaspoon salt*
3   *tablespoons minced fresh chives*

Assemble all ingredients and utensils. In a large pot cook the potatoes in boiling water until tender, about 30 to 35 minutes. Drain and mash the potatoes. Add the milk, yogurt, garlic, and salt. Mash with a potato masher or beat at medium speed using an electric mixer until smooth. Fold in the chives. Yields 8 servings of ½ cup each.

Calories: 72; Fat: 0.1 g; Cholesterol: 0.6 mg; Sodium: 155 mg;
Carbohydrates: 15 g; Fiber: 0.4 g; Diabetic Exchange: 1 starch

PEAS AND PEPPERS

½   pound fresh snow pea pods
1   large red bell pepper, cut into thin strips
¼   cup chopped onion
2   tablespoons slivered almonds, toasted
½   teaspoon salt-free herb and spice blend

Assemble all ingredients and utensils. Wash and string the snow peas. In a large nonstick skillet sauté the snow peas, pepper, and onion until tender. Stir in the toasted almonds and spice blend. Yields 6 servings of ½ cup each.

Calories: 40; Fat: 2 g; Cholesterol: 0 mg; Sodium: 3 mg; Carbohydrates: 5 g; Fiber: 1 g; Diabetic Exchange: ½ starch

SUMMER SQUASH

4   cups sliced yellow squash
½   cup diced onion
¼   cup water
1   bay leaf
½   cup plain nonfat yogurt
1   teaspoon fresh dill

Assemble all ingredients and utensils. Steam the squash, onion, and bay leaf in water for 5 to 7 minutes or cook in boiling water for about 20 minutes or until tender. Drain. Discard the bay leaf. Stir in the yogurt and dill and serve immediately. Yields 4 servings of ½ cup each.

Calories: 48; Fat: 0.4 g; Cholesterol: 0.6 mg; Sodium: 23 mg; Carbohydrates: 9 g; Fiber: 2 g; Diabetic Exchange: 2 vegetable

SPINACH SOUFFLÉ

1   10-ounce package frozen chopped spinach, cooked and drained
3   tablespoons chopped onion
½   cup low-fat cottage cheese
1   teaspoon lemon juice
½   teaspoon nutmeg
½   teaspoon freshly ground black pepper
2   egg whites, stiffly beaten

Assemble all ingredients and utensils. Preheat the oven to 350°. In a food processor or blender purée all of the ingredients except the egg whites. Gently fold in the egg whites. Spoon the mixture into an ungreased soufflé dish or 1½-quart casserole dish. Bake at 350° for 25 to 30 minutes. Serve immediately. Yields 4 servings of ½ cup each.

Calories: 49; Fat: 0.5g; Cholesterol: 1 g; Sodium: 188 mg; Carbohydrates: 5 g; Fiber: 1 g; Diabetic Exchange: 1 vegetable, ½ lower fat meat

MISS DAISY'S SQUASH CASSEROLE

1½ *pounds yellow squash, sliced*
½ *cup chopped onion*
1 *teaspoon reduced-calorie margarine*
1 *tablespoon all-purpose flour*
½ *cup skim milk*
⅓ *cup shredded reduced-fat mild Cheddar cheese*
¼ *teaspoon salt*
¼ *teaspoon ground black pepper*
⅓ *cup chopped green bell pepper*
⅓ *cup toasted whole wheat breadcrumbs*

Assemble all ingredients and utensils. Preheat the oven to 350°. Spray a 1½-quart casserole dish with nonstick cooking spray. In a large pot cook the squash and onion in a small amount of boiling water until tender, about 10 to 12 minutes. Drain.

In a heavy saucepan melt the margarine over medium heat. Add the flour and cook for 1 minute, stirring constantly. Gradually add the milk, stirring until the mixture is thickened. Remove the pan from the heat. Add the Cheddar cheese, salt, and pepper, stirring until the cheese melts. Quickly add the green pepper and squash to the cheese mixture.

Spoon the squash mixture into the prepared dish. Top with the bread-crumbs. Bake at 350° for 45 minutes. Yields 6 servings of ½ cup each.

Calories: 81; Fat: 2 g; Cholesterol: 5 mg; Sodium: 191 mg; Carbohydrates: 12 g; Fiber: 1 g; Diabetic Exchange: ½ starch, 1 vegetable

BAKED PARMESAN TOMATOES

4   *medium tomatoes*
2   *tablespoons very fine whole wheat breadcrumbs*
2   *tablespoons grated Parmesan cheese*
1   *tablespoon minced fresh parsley*
1   *teaspoon dried whole basil*
1   *teaspoon dried whole oregano*
¼   *teaspoon freshly ground black pepper*
2   *teaspoons reduced-calorie margarine, melted*

Assemble all ingredients and utensils. Preheat the oven to 350°. Cut the tops off the tomatoes. Arrange the tomatoes on a nonstick baking sheet. In a small bowl combine the breadcrumbs and remaining ingredients. Top the tomatoes with the mixture. Bake at 350° for 15 to 20 minutes, until the tomatoes are lightly baked, but not too soft. Yields 4 servings.

Calories: 59; Fat: 2 g; Cholesterol: 2 mg; Sodium: 89 mg; Carbohydrates: 8 g; Fiber: 1 g; Diabetic Exchange: 1 vegetable, ½ fat

ITALIAN VEGETABLES

¼   cup chopped onion
1   clove garlic, minced
1   medium zucchini, sliced
1   medium yellow squash, diced
1   green bell pepper; seeded and sliced
2   teaspoons dried leaf oregano
1   cup diced fresh mushrooms
1   large tomato, cut into wedges
2   tablespoons freshly grated Parmesan cheese

Assemble all ingredients and utensils. In a large nonstick skillet sauté the onion and garlic until the onion is tender. Stir in the zucchini, yellow squash, green pepper, oregano, and mushrooms. Cover and cook over medium heat, stirring frequently, for about 5 minutes or until the squash is tender, but crisp. Stir in the tomato. Cover and cook 1 minute more. Sprinkle with Parmesan cheese and serve immediately. Yields 6 servings of 1 cup each.

Calories: 44; Fat: 1 g; Cholesterol: 1 mg; Sodium: 37 mg;
Carbohydrates: 8 g; Fiber: 1 g; Diabetic Exchange: 2 vegetable

~ 14 ~

SAUCES AND CONDIMENTS

RED PEPPER SAUCE

Great over chicken, fish, or pasta.

4	*medium red bell peppers*
1	*tablespoon apple juice concentrate*
1	*teaspoon minced garlic*
¼	*teaspoon salt*
¼	*teaspoon ground black pepper*

Assemble all ingredients and utensils. Preheat the broiler. Place the peppers about 3 inches from the heat and broil, turning occasionally, until the skin blisters and is slightly blackened. When the peppers are cool enough to handle, trim off the tops and remove the seeds and peel. In a blender or food processor combine the peppers and remaining ingredients, and purée. Yields 4 servings of 2 to 3 tablespoons each.

Calories: 30; Fat: 0.4g; Cholesterol: 0 mg; Sodium: 138 mg;
Carbohydrates: 7 g; Fiber: 0.8 g; Diabetic Exchange: 1 vegetable

LEMON BUTTER

Excellent served with fish or steamed veggies.

½   cup reduced-calorie margarine
¼   cup fresh lemon juice
1   tablespoon minced fresh parsley
⅛   teaspoon ground white pepper

Assemble all ingredients and utensils. In a saucepan combine all of the ingredients. Cook over medium heat until the margarine is melted. The Lemon Butter will keep covered in the refrigerator for 14 days. Yields ½ cup or 8 servings of 1 tablespoon each.

Calories: 79; Fat: 9 g; Cholesterol: 0 mg; Sodium: 143 mg;
Carbohydrates: 1 g; Fiber: 0 g; Diabetic Exchange: 2 fat

BASIC WHITE SAUCE

2   tablespoons reduced-calorie margarine
2   tablespoons cornstarch
2½ cups skim milk
¼   teaspoon ground black or white pepper

Assemble all ingredients and utensils. In a medium saucepan melt the margarine. Remove the pan from the heat. Mix the cornstarch with ¼ cup of milk until smooth. Stir the cornstarch into the melted margarine. Return the saucepan to the stove over low heat. Gradually add the remaining milk, stirring constantly until thickened. Yields 1¼ cups or 20 servings of 1 tablespoon each.

Calories: 19; Fat: 0.7 g; Cholesterol: 0.6 mg; Sodium: 21 mg;
Carbohydrates: 2 g; Fiber: 0 g; Diabetic Exchange: free

PARMESAN CHEESE SAUCE

Excellent for rice, potatoes, or steamed veggies.

½ cup low-fat cottage cheese
2   tablespoons grated Parmesan cheese
1   tablespoon reduced-calorie margarine
2   tablespoons cornstarch mixed with 2 tablespoons water
1   cup skim milk
¼   teaspoon ground thyme
¼   teaspoon ground oregano

Assemble all ingredients and utensils. In a small bowl combine the cottage cheese and Parmesan. Set the mixture aside. In a saucepan melt the margarine over low heat. Stir in the cornstarch mixture and cook until the mixture begins to thicken. Slowly add the skim milk and herbs. Stir constantly over medium heat until the sauce is smooth. Add the cheese mixture and stir until the cheese melts. Simmer for 2 to 3 minutes more. Yields 2 cups or 32 servings of 1 tablespoon each.

Calories: 11; Fat: 0.4 g; Cholesterol: 0.5 mg; Sodium: 29 mg;
Carbohydrates: 1 g; Fiber: 0 g; Diabetic Exchange: free

SWEET AND SOUR SAUCE

Excellent way to prepare chicken or shrimp.

1   tablespoon reduced-calorie margarine
1   tablespoon cornstarch
1   cup skim milk
2   teaspoons dry mustard
2   teaspoons brown sugar
2   teaspoons white wine vinegar

Assemble all ingredients and utensils. In a medium saucepan melt the margarine over medium heat. In a small bowl mix the cornstarch with 2 tablespoons skim milk until smooth. Add the cornstarch mixture to the saucepan, stirring until the mixture bubbles. Add the remaining milk and other ingredients and cook, stirring constantly, until smooth and creamy. Yields 1¼ cups or 20 servings of 1 tablespoon each.

Calories: 13; Fat: 0.5 g; Cholesterol: 0.2 mg; Sodium: 9 mg; Carbohydrates: 2 g; Fiber: 0 g; Diabetic Exchange: free

BARBECUE SAUCE

Great on chicken, beef, or pork.

½   cup water
¼   cup white wine (optional)
3   tablespoons lemon juice
1   tablespoon Dijon mustard
¼   cup catsup
2   tablespoons tomato paste
2   tablespoons Worcestershire sauce
½   teaspoon ground black pepper
½   teaspoon paprika

Assemble all ingredients and utensils. In a small saucepan combine all of the ingredients. Bring the mixture to a boil, then reduce the heat and simmer for 30 minutes, stirring frequently. Yields 1 cup or 16 servings of 1 tablespoon each.

Calories: 13; Fat: 0.1 g; Cholesterol: 0 mg; Sodium: 115 mg; Carbohydrates: 2 g; Fiber: 0 g; Diabetic Exchange: free

HORSERADISH TOPPER

A must for baked potatoes.

¾   cup low-fat cottage cheese
3   tablespoons prepared horseradish
¼   cup plain nonfat yogurt
1   teaspoon Worcestershire sauce
1   tablespoon chopped fresh chives

Assemble all ingredients and utensils. In blender or food processor combine all of the ingredients and process until smooth. Chill. Will keep refrigerated for up to a week. Yields 1⅓ cups or 21 servings of 1 tablespoon each.

Calories: 8; Fat: 0.1 g; Cholesterol: 0.4 mg; Sodium: 40 mg; Carbohydrates: 1 g; Fiber: 0 g; Diabetic Exchange: free

TARTAR SAUCE

A must with fish.

1   cup reduced-calorie mayonnaise
3   tablespoons pickle relish
1   tablespoon prepared mustard
2   tablespoons freshly squeezed lemon juice
2   tablespoons white vinegar

Assemble all ingredients and utensils. Combine all ingredients and chill.
Yields 1½ cups or 24 servings of 1 tablespoon each.

Calories: 18; Fat: 1 g; Cholesterol: 5 mg; Sodium: 34 mg;
Carbohydrates: 1 g; Fiber: 0 g; Diabetic Exchange: free

CILANTRO PESTO

Serve with pasta or as a potato topper.

6   tablespoons water
2   cloves garlic, minced
¼   cup Parmesan cheese
3   cups cilantro sprigs
¼   cup pine nuts
1   tablespoon safflower oil
¼   teaspoon salt
1   cup chopped fresh parsley

Assemble all ingredients and utensils. In a food processor or blender combine all of the ingredients and purée. Scrape the sides down from time to time and pulse again. Will keep refrigerated up to a week or will freeze.
Yields 1 cup or 16 servings of 1 tablespoon each.

Calories: 28; Fat: 3 g; Cholesterol: 1 mg; Sodium: 58 mg;
Carbohydrates: 1 g; Fiber: 0 g; Diabetic Exchange: ½ fat

BASIL PESTO

Serve with pasta.

2   cups fresh basil leaves
2   cloves garlic
½   cup pine nuts
3   tablespoons grated Romano cheese
5   tablespoons grated Parmesan cheese
5   tablespoons olive oil

Assemble all ingredients and utensils. Wash the basil leaves carefully and pat them dry. In a food processor or blender purée the ingredients in the order listed except the oil. Slowly add the oil in a thin stream. As soon as all of the oil is added, scrape down the sides of processor or blender and transfer the pesto to a bowl. Refrigerate. Yields 1½ cups or 24 servings of 1 tablespoon each.

Calories: 57; Fat: 5 g; Cholesterol: 2 mg; Sodium: 28 mg; Carbohydrates: 3 g; Fiber: 0 g; Diabetic Exchange: 1 fat

HOMEMADE CATSUP

1   tablespoon sugar
1½ teaspoons white wine vinegar
1   6-ounce can tomato paste
2   teaspoons Worcestershire sauce
⅛   teaspoon Tabasco sauce
2   cloves garlic, minced
½   teaspoon ground black pepper
½   cup water

Assemble all ingredients and utensils. In a bowl combine the sugar and vinegar. Mix well. Add the remaining ingredients except the water, and mix well. Add water to the desired thickness. Refrigerate. Yields 1 cup or 16 servings of 1 tablespoon each.

Calories: 13; Fat: 0.1 g; Cholesterol: 0 mg; Sodium: 94 mg;
Carbohydrates: 3 g; Fiber: 0 g; Diabetic Exchange: free

MARINARA SAUCE

Serve with pasta, chicken, or fish.

¼   *medium yellow onion, chopped*
3   *cloves garlic, minced*
1   *teaspoon vegetable oil*
1   *28-ounce can Italian plum tomatoes, chopped*
1   *teaspoon dried leaf oregano*
1   *teaspoon dried leaf basil*

Assemble all ingredients and utensils. In a medium saucepan sauté the onion and garlic in oil until soft. Add the tomatoes and herbs and bring the mixture to a boil. Simmer for 1 hour and 30 minutes or until the desired thickness. Yields 3 cups or 6 servings of ½ cup each.

Calories: 38; Fat: 1 g; Cholesterol: 0 mg; Sodium: 217 mg;
Carbohydrates: 7 g; Fiber: 1 g; Diabetic Exchange: 1 vegetable

COCKTAIL SAUCE

1   *cup catsup (see recipe for homemade on the previous page)*
1   *tablespoon lemon juice*
2   *teaspoons prepared horseradish*
2   *teaspoons red wine vinegar*
¼   *teaspoon freshly ground black pepper*

Assemble all ingredients and utensils. In a medium bowl combine all of the ingredients. Mix well. Cover and refrigerate. Yields 18 servings of 1 tablespoon each.

Calories: 12; Fat: 0.1 g; Cholesterol: 0 mg; Sodium: 84 mg;
Carbohydrates: 3 g; Fiber: 0 g; Diabetic Exchange: free

SOUTHWESTERN SALSA

Great with chicken or fish.

3½ cups chopped fresh tomatoes
1   4-ounce can chopped green chilies, drained
½   cup finely chopped purple onion
⅓   cup chopped fresh cilantro
2   tablespoons lime juice
1   large clove garlic, minced
1   teaspoon dried leaf oregano
½   teaspoon ground cumin
¼   teaspoon salt

Assemble all ingredients and utensils. In a small bowl combine all of the ingredients. Mix well. Cover and refrigerate. Yields 4 cups or 48 servings of 1 tablespoon each.

> Calories: 4; Fat: 0.1 g; Cholesterol: 0 mg; Sodium: 29 mg;
> Carbohydrates: 1 g; Fiber: 0.2 g; Diabetic Exchange: free

TOMATO SALSA

1¼ cups canned Italian plum tomatoes, drained
1   celery stalk, diced
¼   cup chopped green onions
1   teaspoon minced garlic
1   tablespoon fresh lime juice
2   tablespoons chopped fresh cilantro
¼   teaspoon hot red pepper flakes
¼   teaspoon freshly ground black pepper

Assemble all ingredients and utensils. Coarsely chop the tomatoes. In a large bowl combine the tomatoes and remaining ingredients. Cover and chill. Yields 1½ cups or 6 servings of 2 to 3 tablespoons each.

Calories: 14; Fat: 0.2 g; Cholesterol: 0 mg; Sodium: 88 mg; Carbohydrates: 3 g; Fiber: 0.4 g; Diabetic Exchange: free

CHEESE SAUCE

½   cup instant nonfat dry milk powder
2   tablespoons all-purpose flour
1½ cups water
¼   teaspoon salt
¼   teaspoon dry mustard
⅓   cup shredded low-fat Cheddar cheese

Assemble all ingredients and utensils. In a saucepan combine the dry milk powder, flour, and water. Heat, stirring, until smooth and partially thickened. Add the salt, mustard, and low-fat Cheddar cheese, and stir constantly until the mixture is the desired thickness. Yields 1¼ cup or 20 servings of 1 tablespoon each.

Calories: 14; Fat: 0.4 g; Cholesterol: 2 mg; Sodium: 51 mg; Carbohydrates: 2 g; Fiber: 0 g; Diabetic Exchange: free

15

DESSERTS

TRADITIONAL CHEESECAKE

1   cup graham cracker crumbs
¼   cup reduced-calorie margarine
1   32-ounce carton low-fat vanilla yogurt
2   tablespoons sugar
3   tablespoons cornstarch
½   teaspoon vanilla extract
½   teaspoon almond extract
2   large eggs
    Fresh fruit for garnish, optional

Assemble all ingredients and utensils. Preheat the oven to 425°. In a small bowl combine the graham cracker crumbs and margarine. Press the mixture into the bottom of a 9-inch springform pan. In a medium bowl combine the yogurt, sugar, cornstarch, vanilla, almond extract, and eggs. Mix with a wire whip until well blended. Spoon the batter into the pan. Bake at 425° for 50 to 60 minutes or until the center is set. Cool and refrigerate until serving time. Yields 1 cake or 12 servings.

Calories: 120; Fat: 5 g; Cholesterol: 50 mg; Sodium: 129 mg;
Carbohydrates: 14 g; Fiber: 0.1 g; Diabetic Exchange: 1 fat, ½ starch, ½ milk

CARROT CAKE

¾ cup safflower oil

¾ cup sugar

2 large eggs

1 cup grated carrots

2½ cups all-purpose flour

1 tablespoon baking powder

1 teaspoon ground cinnamon

½ teaspoon ground allspice

¼ teaspoon ground cloves

1 cup orange juice

½ cup finely chopped pecans

  Cream Cheese Frosting, optional (see recipe, p.254)

Assemble all ingredients and utensils. Preheat the oven to 325°. Grease and flour a 10-inch tube or bundt pan. In a large mixing bowl beat together the oil, sugar, and eggs until soft. Stir in the carrots. In a separate bowl combine the flour, baking powder, cinnamon, allspice, and cloves. Add the dry ingredients to the egg mixture alternately with the orange juice. Fold in the pecans. Spoon the batter into the prepared pan. Bake at 325° for 55 to 60 minutes or until a toothpick inserted in the center comes out clean. Cool 5 minutes before removing from the pan. Lightly ice the top of the cake with Cream Cheese Frosting, optional. Yields 16 servings.

Calories: 242 (with frosting: 253); Fat: 10 g (with frosting: 14 g); Cholesterol: 34 mg (with frosting: 36 mg); Sodium: 92 mg (with frosting: 219 mg); Carbohydrates: 27 g (with frosting: 30 g); Fiber: 0.2 g (with frosting: 2 g); Diabetic Exchange: 1½ starch, 2 fat, 1 fruit

YUMMY CHOCOLATE CAKE

¾ cup reduced-calorie margarine, softened
¼ cup sugar
½ cup liquid egg substitute at room temperature
   Liquid sugar substitute equivalent to ⅓ cup sugar
1 tablespoon vanilla
2 cups cake flour
2 teaspoons baking powder
¼ cup instant nonfat dry milk
⅓ cup unsweetened cocoa
1 cup water, room temperature
   Delicious Chocolate Sauce, optional (see recipe, p. 260)

Assemble all ingredients and utensils. Preheat the oven to 350°. Grease a 9-inch square pan with a small amount of reduced-calorie margarine. In a large mixing bowl beat together the margarine and sugar until light and fluffy. Add the egg substitute, sugar substitute, and vanilla, and beat at medium speed for 30 seconds. In a separate bowl combine the remaining dry ingredients. Add the dry mixture and water alternately to the margarine mixture, mixing until smooth. Spread the batter evenly in the prepared pan. Bake at 350° for 30 to 35 minutes, or until a toothpick inserted in the center comes out clean. Yields 16 servings.

Calories: 111; Fat: 5 g; Cholesterol: 0.3 mg; Sodium: 102 mg; Carbohydrates: 15 g; Fiber: 0 g; Diabetic Exchange: 1 fat, 1 starch

GINGERBREAD

1½ cups all-purpose flour

¼ cup sugar

1 teaspoon baking soda

⅛ teaspoon salt

2 teaspoons ground ginger

1 teaspoon ground cinnamon

½ teaspoon ground cloves

⅔ cup unsweetened applesauce

⅓ cup molasses

3 tablespoons safflower oil

1 egg, lightly beaten

Lemon Sauce, optional (see recipe, p. 261)

Assemble all ingredients and utensils. Preheat the oven to 350°. Spray a 9-inch square baking pan with nonstick cooking spray. In a large mixing bowl combine the dry ingredients. Stir well. In a small bowl combine the applesauce, molasses, oil, and egg. Add to the flour mixture, stirring well. Spoon the batter into the prepared pan. Bake at 350° for 20 to 25 minutes or until the cake tests done. Serve hot with Lemon Sauce, if desired. Yields 12 servings.

Calories: 140 (with sauce: 177); Fat: 4 g (with sauce: 7 g); Cholesterol: 23 mg (with sauce: 23 mg); Sodium: 100 mg (with sauce: 175 mg); Carbohydrates: 24 g (with sauce: 27 g); Fiber: 0.1 g (with sauce: 0.1 g); Diabetic Exchange: 1½ starch, 1 fat (with sauce: 1½ starch, 2 fat)

PUMPKIN MOUSSE PIE

10 vanilla wafers, crushed
1   tablespoon margarine, melted
1   package unflavored gelatin
1½ cups evaporated skim milk
½   cup part-skim ricotta cheese
1¼ cups canned pumpkin
10 packages sugar substitute
1   teaspoon vanilla extract
2   teaspoons pumpkin pie spice
1   cup Homemade Whipped Topping (see recipe, p. 253)

Assemble all ingredients and utensils. In a blender or food processor process the vanilla wafers. In an ungreased 8-inch pie plate combine the crumbs and the melted margarine. Press the mixture into the prepared pie plate and freeze for 1 hour.

In a small bowl sprinkle the gelatin over ½ cup of evaporated milk. Let the mixture stand for 10 minutes. Gently heat the mixture until the gelatin dissolves. In a food processor or blender combine the milk-gelatin mixture with the ricotta, pumpkin, sugar substitute, vanilla, pumpkin pie spice, and remaining milk. Pour the filling into the pie crust and chill.

Top each slice of pie with 1 tablespoon of Homemade Whipped Topping. Yields 8 servings.

Calories: 124; Fat: 4 g; Cholesterol: 9 mg; Sodium: 121 mg; Carbohydrates: 16 g; Fiber: 0 g; Diabetic Exchange: 1 low-fat milk

CHOCOLATE MOUSSE PIE

10 *vanilla wafers, crushed*
1 *tablespoon reduced-calorie margarine*
1 *package unflavored gelatin*
1½ *cups nonfat milk*
¾ *cup part-skim ricotta cheese*
½ *cup unsweetened cocoa*
10 *packages sugar substitute*
2 *teaspoons vanilla extract*
1 *envelope reduced-calorie whipped topping mix*

Assemble all ingredients and utensils. In a small bowl mix the wafers with the margarine. Press them into the bottom and sides of a 9-inch pie pan. Freeze for 1 hour. In a small saucepan sprinkle the gelatin over ½ cup of nonfat milk. Let stand for 10 minutes, then heat over low heat until the gelatin is dissolved. In a medium bowl blend together the ricotta cheese, cocoa powder, sugar substitute, vanilla, gelatin mixture, and the remaining milk. Pour the filling into the pie crust and chill.

Prepare the whipped topping according to the package directions. Spread over the top of the chilled pie mixture. Yields 8 servings.

Calories: 107; Fat: 5 g; Cholesterol: 10 mg; Sodium: 84 mg; Carbohydrates: 12 g; Fiber: 0 g; Diabetic Exchange: 1 low-fat milk

CHERRY PIE

2 16-ounce cans unsweetened red cherries
1 cup liquid from cherries
1 tablespoon cornstarch
⅛ teaspoon almond flavoring
   Sugar substitute equal to 1 cup sugar
1 prebaked Never Fail Pie Crust (see recipe, p. 242)
   Homemade Whipped Topping, optional (see recipe, p. 253)

Assemble all ingredients and utensils. Drain the cherries well, reserving 1 cup of liquid. In a saucepan combine the liquid and the cornstarch. Cook and stir over medium heat until thickened and transparent. Remove the pan from the heat and add the almond flavoring, sugar substitute, and cherries. Cool. Spread the filling in the crust and chill another 15 minutes before serving. Cut into 8 slices and top with 1 or 2 tablespoons of whipped topping before serving. Yields 1 9-inch pie or 8 servings.

Calories: 186; Fat: 8 g; Cholesterol: 0 mg; Sodium: 82 mg; Carbohydrates: 27 g; Fiber: 0.1 g; Diabetic Exchange: 1 starch, 1 fat, 1 fruit

MISS DAISY'S KEY LIME PIE

1 *envelope unflavored gelatin*
3 *tablespoons fresh lime juice*
½ *cup boiling water*
9 *individual sugar substitute packets*
1 *cup evaporated skim milk*
1 *teaspoon vanilla extract*
   Juice of 1½ limes (3 tablespoons)
1 *drop green food coloring, optional*
1 *9-inch Graham Cracker Crust (see recipe, p. 242)*
   Low-calorie whipped topping, optional
   Lime slices

Assemble all ingredients and utensils. In a medium bowl sprinkle the gelatin over the lime juice and let the mixture stand for 1 minute. Add the boiling water and sweetener to the gelatin mixture and stir until the gelatin is dissolved. Refrigerate until slightly thickened, about 45 minutes. In a separate bowl combine the milk and vanilla, and freeze for 30 minutes. Remove the milk from the freezer and whip with an electric mixer until stiff. Stir the lime juice and food coloring into the whipped milk. Slowly blend the gelatin mixture into the whipped milk. Spoon the filling into the crust. Chill until firm. Garnish with lime slices and 2 tablespoons whipped topping per slice. Yields 12 servings.

Calories: 81; Fat: 2 g; Cholesterol: 0.3 mg; Sodium: 123 mg; Carbohydrates: 13 g; Fiber: 0.1 g; Diabetic Exchange: 1 starch

MISS DAISY'S LEMON MERINGUE PIE

⅔ cup sugar
⅓ cup cornstarch
2 cups skim milk
½ cup frozen egg substitute, thawed
1 tablespoon grated lemon rind
⅓ cup fresh lemon juice
1 9-inch Never Fail Pie Crust (see recipe, p. 242)
4 egg whites
½ teaspoon cream of tartar
½ teaspoon vanilla extract
2 tablespoons sugar

Assemble all ingredients and utensils. In a saucepan combine ⅔ cup sugar and the cornstarch; gradually stir in the milk. Cook over medium heat, stirring constantly. Remove the pan from the heat. Slowly stir one-fourth of the hot mixture into the egg substitute. Add the egg substitute mixture back into the pan, stirring constantly. Cook over medium heat, stirring constantly until thickened. Remove the pan from the heat. Stir in the lemon rind and juice. Spoon the mixture into the pastry shell.

In a small mixing bowl beat the egg whites, cream of tartar, and vanilla with an electric mixer at high speed. Gradually stir in 2 tablespoons sugar and continue beating until stiff peaks form. Spread the meringue over the hot filling. Bake at 325° for 15 to 20 minutes or until golden brown. Yields 1 9-inch pie or 8 servings.

Calories: 266; Fat: 8 g; Cholesterol: 1 mg; Sodium: 171 mg;
Carbohydrates: 40 g; Fiber: 0 g; Diabetic Exchange: not recommended

ORANGE–CREAM PIE

2   *tablespoons reduced-calorie margarine*
2   *tablespoons orange marmalade*
1¼ *cups graham cracker crumbs*
½   *teaspoon cinnamon*
3   *cups orange sherbet, softened*
3   *cups frozen nonfat vanilla yogurt, softened*

Assemble all ingredients and utensils. Preheat the oven to 350°. Spray a 9-inch pie pan with nonstick cooking spray. In a saucepan over low heat melt the margarine and orange marmalade. Stir in the graham cracker crumbs and cinnamon, and mix well. Press the crumbs into the bottom and sides of the prepared pan. Bake at 350° for 8 to 10 minutes or until lightly browned. Cool.

In a separate bowl, fold the sherbet and yogurt together until combined. Spoon the mixture into the baked crust. Freeze for 1 hour to 1 hour and 30 minutes until firm. Remove the pie from the freezer 10 minutes before cutting. Garnish each serving with an orange slice. Yields 10 servings.

Calories: 210; Fat: 6 g; Cholesterol: 3 mg; Sodium: 160 mg; Carbohydrates: 41 g; Fiber: 1 g; Diabetic Exchange: 1½ fruit, 1 fat, 1 starch

STRAWBERRY PIE

1   cup crushed chocolate wafers
1   teaspoon reduced-calorie margarine
1   cup plain low-fat yogurt
1   cup part-skim ricotta cheese
2   teaspoons sugar
1   teaspoon vanilla extract
1   package unflavored gelatin
1   tablespoon cold water
3   tablespoons boiling water
1   cup sliced fresh strawberries

Assemble all ingredients and utensils. In a small bowl combine the chocolate wafer crumbs and margarine. Press into a 9-inch pie pan and freeze
for 1 hour. In a medium bowl mix the yogurt, ricotta cheese, sugar, and
vanilla with an electric mixer. Soften the gelatin in 1 tablespoon of cold
water. Stir in 3 tablespoons of boiling water. Add the gelatin mixture to
the yogurt mixture and blend well. Arrange the sliced strawberries in the
pie crust. Pour the yogurt mixture over the strawberries and spread
evenly. Chill for several hours, until firm. Garnish with additional strawberries before serving. Yields 12 servings.

Calories: 97; Fat: 4 g; Cholesterol: 9 mg; Sodium: 118 mg;
Carbohydrates: 12 g; Fiber: 0.6 g; Diabetic Exchange: 1 starch, ½ fat

GRAHAM CRACKER CRUST

8   2½-inch square graham crackers, crushed
3   tablespoons reduced-calorie margarine
2   tablespoons sugar

Assemble all ingredients and utensils. Preheat the oven to 350°. In a small bowl combine all of the ingredients. Press the crumbs evenly around the bottom and sides of a 9-inch pie pan. Bake at 350° for 5 to 7 minutes. Fill as desired. Yields 1 9-inch pie crust or 8 servings.

Calories: 85; Fat: 3 g; Cholesterol: 0 mg; Sodium: 147 mg; Carbohydrates: 13 g; Fiber: 0.1 g; Diabetic Exchange: 1 bread

NEVER–FAIL PIE CRUST

⅓   cup margarine, softened
1   cup all-purpose flour
¼   cup ice water
¼   teaspoon salt
1   egg white
1½   teaspoons white vinegar

Assemble all ingredients and utensils. In a small bowl cut the margarine into the flour until the mixture resembles coarse meal. In a small bowl combine the water, salt, egg white, and vinegar. Mix well, then add the liquids to the flour mixture. Mix lightly with a fork until the pastry forms a ball. Refrigerate until ready to use.

Roll the crust out on a floured surface to form a circle. Press the pastry into a 9-inch pie tin and prick the bottom with the tines of a fork. Bake at

425° for 12 to 15 minutes or until lightly brown, or fill the unbaked crust with the desired filling. Yields 1 9-inch pie crust or 8 servings.

Calories: 126; Fat: 8 g; Cholesterol: 0 mg; Sodium: 73 mg; Carbohydrates: 12 g; Fiber: 0 g; Diabetic Exchange: 1 starch, 1 fat

DOUBLE CHOCOLATE COOKIES

¾   *cup safflower oil*
⅔   *cup sugar*
1   *large egg*
1   *teaspoon baking powder*
½   *teaspoon baking soda*
1½ *cups all-purpose flour*
⅓   *cup unsweetened cocoa*
¼   *cup finely chopped pecans*
½   *cup semisweet chocolate chips*

Assemble all ingredients and utensils. Preheat the oven to 350°. Spray a baking sheet with nonstick cooking spray. In a large mixing bowl beat together the oil, sugar, and egg. Add the remaining ingredients and stir to blend well. Let the dough stand for 10 minutes. Drop by spoonfuls about 1 inch apart onto the prepared baking sheet. Bake at 350° for 12 to 15 minutes until browned. Yields 36 medium-size cookies.

Calories: 95; Fat: 6 g; Cholesterol: 8 mg; Sodium: 23 mg; Carbohydrates: 10 g; Fiber: 0.1 g; Diabetic Exchange: ½ starch, 1 fat

PEANUT BUTTER COOKIES

½ cup reduced-fat smooth peanut butter
¼ cup safflower oil
1 cup packed brown sugar
2 teaspoons vanilla extract
1 large egg
1½ cups whole wheat flour
2 teaspoons baking soda

Assemble all ingredients and utensils. Preheat the oven to 350°. In a large mixing bowl beat together the peanut butter and oil with an electric mixer until soft. Add the brown sugar, vanilla, and egg. Beat well. Add the flour and soda, and mix thoroughly. Shape the dough into 24 medium-size balls and place about 1 inch apart on an ungreased baking sheet. Flatten with a fork. Bake at 350° for 12 to 15 minutes. Yields 24 cookies.

Calories: 103; Fat: 5 g; Cholesterol: 11 mg; Sodium: 97 mg;
Carbohydrates: 14 g; Fiber: 0.4 g; Diabetic Exchange: 1 starch, ½ fat

ORANGE MERINGUE COOKIES

3 egg whites, room temperature
¼ teaspoon cream of tartar
¼ cup sugar
⅓ cup sliced almonds
2 tablespoons grated orange rind

Assemble all ingredients and utensils. Preheat the oven to 250°. Spray 2 cookie sheets with nonstick cooking spray. In a large bowl beat the egg whites with an electric mixer until foamy. Add the cream of tartar and beat on high until soft peaks form. Beat in 1 tablespoon of sugar at a time, beating to stiff peaks. Remove the beaters from the mixing bowl and gently fold in the almonds and orange rind. Drop the meringue by heaping table-spoons onto the prepared cookie sheets.

Bake at 250° for 1 hour. Turn off the oven and do not open the door for another hour. Then remove the cookies from the oven and cool completely. Store the cookies in a tightly covered container. Serve as a cookie or as a shell for fresh fruit. Yields 24 servings of 1 cookie each.

Calories: 22; Fat: 1 g; Cholesterol: 0 mg; Sodium: 9 mg; Carbohydrates: 3 g; Fiber: 1 g; Diabetic Exchange: free

DA'S SPRITZ COOKIES

¾ *cup reduced-calorie margarine*
½ *cup sugar*
2 *large egg yolks*
½ *teaspoon almond extract*
½ *teaspoon vanilla extract*
2 *cups all-purpose flour*
½ *teaspoon baking powder*
   Finely chopped pecans

Assemble all ingredients and utensils. Preheat the oven to 375°. In a large mixing bowl beat the margarine, sugar, and egg yolks with an electric mixer until light and fluffy. Add the extracts. Gradually blend in the flour and baking powder. Chill the dough for several hours.

Fill a cookie press with the dough. Form cookies on an ungreased cookie sheet and sprinkle lightly with pecans. Bake at 375° for about 10 minutes or until browned. Cool. Yields 48 medium cookies.

Calories: 44; Fat: 2 g; Cholesterol: 11 mg; Sodium: 17 mg; Carbohydrates: 6 g; Fiber: 0 g; Diabetic Exchange: ½ starch

VANILLA PUDDING

2   *cups skim milk*
2   *tablespoons cornstarch*
3   *tablespoons brown sugar*
1   *tablespoon vanilla extract*

Assemble all ingredients and utensils. In a very heavy saucepan or double boiler combine 1½ cups milk and the cornstarch. Stir well. Heat the mixture. Add the remaining milk to the original mixture. Stir in the remaining ingredients and cook over very low heat until thickened, about 20 minutes. Pour into individual bowls and refrigerate. Yields 4 servings of ½ cup each.

Calories: 82; Fat: 0.2 g; Cholesterol: 2 mg; Sodium: 65 mg; Carbohydrates: 16 g; Fiber: 0 g; Diabetic Exchange: ½ milk, ½ starch

BREAD PUDDING

3   *slices whole wheat bread, cubed*
6   *unsweetened pitted dates, chopped*
2   *medium apples, peeled and chopped*
¼   *cup unsweetened apple juice*
1   *egg*
2   *egg whites*
¾   *cup skim milk*
¼   *teaspoon ground cinnamon*
1   *teaspoon vanilla extract*

Assemble all ingredients and utensils. Preheat the oven to 350°. Spray an 8-inch square baking pan with nonstick cooking spray. Place the bread cubes, dates, and apples in the prepared pan. Set the pan aside. In a small mixing bowl beat together the apple juice, egg, egg whites, milk, cinnamon, and vanilla until smooth. Pour the liquid over the bread and fruit mixture in the pan. Bake at 350° for 40 to 45 minutes. Serve warm with low-calorie whipped topping. Yields 6 servings of ½ cup each.

Calories: 112; Fat: 2 g; Cholesterol: 47 mg; Sodium: 111 mg;
Carbohydrates: 21 g; Fiber: 2 g; Diabetic Exchange: ½ starch, 1 fruit

RICE PUDDING

½   cup white rice
¾   cup water
2   cups skim milk
¼   cup sugar
2   teaspoons vanilla extract
½   cup raisins

Assemble all ingredients and utensils. In a medium saucepan cook the rice in the water over medium heat until tender, about 40 to 45 minutes. Add the skim milk and sugar. Cook slowly over low heat until thickened, about 30 minutes. Cool. Add the vanilla and raisins and serve. Yields 6 servings of ½ cup each.

Calories: 153; Fat: 0.3 g; Cholesterol: 2 mg; Sodium: 45 mg;
Carbohydrates: 34 g; Fiber: 0.1 g; Diabetic Exchange: 2 starch

INDIVIDUAL CHOCOLATE PUDDINGS

1   *envelope reduced-calorie whipped topping mix*
2   *tablespoons unsweetened cocoa powder*
½   *cup nonfat milk*
1   *teaspoon vanilla extract*

Assemble all ingredients and utensils. In a mixing bowl combine the topping mix and cocoa. Blend in the milk and vanilla. Beat on high speed for 2 to 3 minutes. Continue beating until light and fluffy. Spoon ½ cup of the mixture into 4 individual bowls. Chill until ready to serve. Top with additional whipped topping if desired. Yields 2 cups or 4 servings of ½ cup each.

Calories: 19; Fat: 0.4 g; Cholesterol: 2 mg; Sodium: 21 mg; Carbohydrates: 2 g; Fiber: 0 g; Diabetic Exchange: 1 serving free

RASPBERRY BOMBE

2   *pints frozen raspberry nonfat yogurt*
1   *pint frozen strawberry nonfat yogurt*
1   *cup Homemade Whipped Topping, (see recipe, p. 253)*
¼   *cup finely chopped dates*
¼   *cup ground or crushed Grape-Nuts cereal*
¼   *teaspoon rum flavoring*
¼   *teaspoon almond flavoring*

Assemble all ingredients and utensils. Chill a 1½-quart salad mold in the freezer. Stir the raspberry yogurt to soften it and spread it on the bottom and sides of the mold. Freeze immediately until firm. Next stir the strawberry yogurt to soften it and place it over the raspberry yogurt. Freeze immediately until firm. In a small bowl combine the whipped topping, dates, Grape-Nuts, and flavorings. Pour the mixture into the mold and spread evenly. Cover with foil. Freeze for several hours. To remove the bombe from the mold, immerse the mold quickly into a small amount of water to loosen. Invert on to a chilled plate and garnish with fresh strawberries. Yields 8 servings of ½ cup each.

Calories: 183; Fat: 0.01 g; Cholesterol: 8 mg; Sodium: 100 mg; Carbohydrates: 43 g; Fiber: 0.2 g; Diabetic Exchange: 3 starch, not recommended

CRANBERRY FREEZE

1 8-ounce carton frozen vanilla nonfat yogurt, thawed
2 16-ounce cans whole berry cranberry sauce
1 15-ounce can crushed pineapple, drained
3 bananas, sliced
   Homemade Whipped Topping (see recipe, p. 253)

Assemble all ingredients and utensils. In a large mixing bowl combine all of the ingredients, blending well. Pour the mixture into a 13 x 9 x 2-inch pan or 16 individual molds. Freeze until firm. Garnish with a tablespoon of Homemade Whipped Topping. Great as a dessert or salad. Yields 16 servings of ½ cup each.

Calories: 131; Fat: 0.1 g; Cholesterol: trace; Sodium: 16 mg; Carbohydrates: 34 g; Fiber: 0.5 g; Diabetic Exchange: 2 fruit

QUICK APPLESAUCE DESSERT

2   cups unsweetened applesauce
1   small package sugar-free lime gelatin
1   6-ounce bottle diet ginger ale
⅓   cup Grape-Nuts, finely chopped
1   teaspoon ground cinnamon

Assemble all ingredients and utensils. In a saucepan heat the applesauce and dissolve the gelatin in the hot applesauce. Add the remaining ingredients and pour into individual serving dishes. Chill until firm. Yields 6 servings of ½ cup each.

Calories: 64; Fat: 0.1 g; Cholesterol: 0 mg; Sodium: 100 mg; Carbohydrates: 15 g; Fiber: 0.9 g; Diabetic Exchange: 1 fruit

PEACH MELBA

½   cup fresh raspberries, puréed
1   packet sugar substitute
3   large peaches, peeled and halved
⅓   cup low-fat vanilla yogurt

Assemble all ingredients and utensils. In a bowl combine the raspberries and sugar substitute. Place each peach half in a serving dish. Spoon 1 tablespoon yogurt over each peach half. Pour the raspberry purée over each serving. Yields 6 servings.

Calories: 32; Fat: 0.3 g; Cholesterol: 0.1 mg; Sodium: 9 mg; Carbohydrates: 7 g; Fiber: 0.8 g; Diabetic Exchange: ½ fruit

GINGERED YOGURT AMBROSIA

½   cup diced oranges
½   cup sliced bananas
½   cup seedless red grapes
1   tablespoon grated fresh ginger
1   cup nonfat yogurt
6   teaspoons grated coconut

Assemble all ingredients and utensils. In a large bowl mix the fruit with
the ginger and yogurt. When ready to serve, sprinkle each serving with
grated coconut. Yields 6 servings of ½ cup each.

Calories: 48; Fat: 0.6 g; Cholesterol: 0.8 mg; Sodium: 30 mg;
Carbohydrates: 9 g; Fiber: 0.3 g; Diabetic Exchange: ½ milk

HOMEMADE WHIPPED TOPPING

½   cup instant dry milk
⅓   cup cold water
1   tablespoon lemon juice
    Dry sugar substitute equal to ¼ cup sugar
2   teaspoons vanilla extract

Assemble all ingredients and utensils. In a small mixing bowl combine the
dry milk and water. Refrigerate for 30 minutes. Beat the mixture with an
electric mixer at high speed for 4 minutes. Add the lemon juice to the
whipped milk and beat at high speed for 4 minutes. Add the sugar substitute gradually into the whipped milk while it is being beaten. Fold the
vanilla extract into the whipped topping mixture. Refrigerate until ready
to use. Yields 24 servings or 3 cups at 2 tablespoons each.

Calories: 8; Fat: 0 g; Cholesterol: 3 mg; Sodium: 8 mg;
Carbohydrates: 1 g; Fiber: 0 g; Diabetic Exchange: free

CREAM CHEESE FROSTING

1   8-ounce package fat-free cream cheese, softened
½   cup reduced-calorie margarine, softened
1   16-ounce box confectioners' sugar
1   teaspoon vanilla extract
1   cup finely chopped pecans
     Skim milk for spreading

Assemble all ingredients and utensils. In a medium bowl beat together the cream cheese and margarine with an electric mixer. Beat in the confectioners' sugar and vanilla extract. Fold in the pecans. Add a small amount of milk as needed to achieve a spreading consistency. Yields 4 cups or 32 servings of 2 tablespoon each.

Calories: 99; Fat: 4 g; Cholesterol: 1 mg; Sodium: 76 mg; Carbohydrates: 15 g; Fiber: 0 g; Diabetic Exchange: 1 fat, ½ starch

ALTERNATIVE CREAM CHEESE TOPPING

1   small box sugar-free vanilla instant pudding
2   cups skim milk
1   teaspoon vanilla extract
6   ounces fat-free cream cheese, softened

Assemble all ingredients and utensils. In a small mixing bowl combine the pudding mix and milk and beat with an electric mixer on low speed until well blended. Stir in the vanilla and add the cream cheese. Increase the speed and beat until smooth and thick. Yields 2½ cups or 20 servings of 2 tablespoons each.

Calories: 21; Fat: 0.1 g; Cholesterol: 2 mg; Sodium: 127 mg; Carbohydrates: 3 grams; Fiber: 0 g; Diabetic Exchange: ½ milk

CHOCOLATE MOUSSE

3   *egg whites*
1   *envelope unflavored gelatin*
1   *tablespoon cold water*
1   *cup boiling water*
½   *cup part-skim ricotta cheese*
½   *cup skim milk*
2   *tablespoons unsweetened cocoa*
¼   *cup sugar*

Assemble all ingredients and utensils. In a food processor or blender combine the egg whites, gelatin, and cold water. Process until the mixture is blended. Let the mixture stand until the gelatin softens, about 1 minute. Add the boiling water and blend until the gelatin is dissolved, about 30 seconds. Add the ricotta cheese, skim milk, cocoa, and sugar. Blend another minute until smooth. Pour into 8 small dessert dishes or a large bowl and chill until set. Yields 8 servings of ½ cup each.

Calories: 63; Fat: 1 g; Cholesterol: 5 mg; Sodium: 47 mg; Carbohydrates: 9 g; Fiber: 0 g; Diabetic Exchange: ½ milk

APPLE-GINGER MOUSSE

1   *3.4-ounce package sugar-free instant vanilla pudding and pie filling*
1   *cup skim milk*
½   *cup unsweetened applesauce*
¼   *teaspoon ground cinnamon*
1   *cup nondairy whipped topping*
¾   *cup finely crushed gingersnap cookies*
     Apple slices and whipped topping for garnish

Assemble all ingredients and utensils. In a medium bowl combine the pudding, milk, applesauce, and cinnamon, and mix according to the pudding package directions. Fold in 1 cup of whipped topping. In 8 serving dishes, layer the pudding mixture with the crushed gingersnaps. Refrigerate for at least 30 minutes before serving. Garnish each serving with 1 teaspoon of topping and an apple slice. Yields 8 servings of 4 ounces each.

Calories: 45; Fat: 0.1 g; Cholesterol: 0.1 mg; Sodium: 184 mg; Carbohydrates: 9 g; Fiber: 0.5; Diabetic Exchange: ½ starch

HONEY BANANA SOUFFLÉ

3   medium bananas, ripe but not mushy
2   tablespoons lemon juice
2   tablespoons honey
2   tablespoons water
1   tablespoon cornstarch
¾   cup skim milk
2   Egg Beaters egg substitute
2   egg whites
2   teaspoons vanilla extract

Assemble all ingredients and utensils. Preheat the oven to 350°. Peel and slice the bananas. Sprinkle the bananas with lemon juice. In a saucepan mix the honey, water, and cornstarch. Add the milk and mix well. Stir and cook over medium heat until thickened. Add ⅓ cup of the hot mixture to the egg beaters, then add the egg beaters mixture back into the pan. Stir in the sliced bananas. With a wire whisk or mixer beat the egg whites until they stand in stiff peaks. Fold the egg whites into the custard mixture along with the vanilla. Turn the mixture into a 1½-quart soufflé dish. Place the dish in a pan of hot water. Bake at 350° for 1 hour or until firm. Yields 6 servings of ½ cup each.

Calories: 114; Fat: 1 g; Cholesterol: trace; Sodium: 71 mg; Carbohydrates: 23 g; Fiber: 0.8 g; Diabetic Exchange: 1 fruit, ½ skim milk

APPLE CRISP

4   baking apples, sliced
1   tablespoon lemon juice
½   teaspoon cinnamon
1   tablespoon whole wheat flour
⅓   cup raisins
¾   cup water
1   cup rolled oats
¼   cup whole wheat flour
1   teaspoon cinnamon
1   tablespoon brown sugar
2   teaspoons reduced-calorie margarine, melted

Assemble all ingredients and utensils. Preheat the oven to 375°. Spray an 8-inch square baking dish with nonstick cooking spray. In a bowl combine the apples, lemon juice, ½ teaspoon cinnamon, 1 tablespoon whole wheat flour, and raisins. Toss to coat the apples. Spoon the apples into the prepared baking dish. Pour the water over all. Set the pan aside.

In a separate bowl combine the oats, ¼ cup whole wheat flour, 1 teaspoon cinnamon, brown sugar, and margarine. Spread the topping over the apples. Cover. Bake at 375° for 15 minutes. Remove the cover; stir, and bake for 15 to 20 minutes more or until the apples are done. Yields 6 servings of ⅔ cup each.

Calories: 162; Fat: 2 g; Cholesterol: 0 mg; Sodium: 9 mg;
Carbohydrates: 36 g; Fiber: 4 g; Diabetic Exchange: ½ fruit, 1 starch

ANGEL TRIFLE

3   cups buttermilk

2   envelopes unflavored gelatin

⅓   cup sugar

1½ ounce envelope dessert topping mix

½   cup cold low-fat milk

1   12-ounce package frozen whole strawberries or raspberries, thawed, very well drained

1   8-inch angel food cake, torn into bite-sized pieces

Assemble all ingredients and utensils. In a saucepan combine 1½ cups of the buttermilk; sprinkle with gelatin. Let the gelatin soften for 5 minutes or until the gelatin is dissolved, stirring constantly. Add the sugar and cook until dissolved. Remove the pan from the heat. Stir in the remaining buttermilk. Refrigerate until chilled. In a mixing bowl combine the dessert topping mix and milk, and beat with an electric mixer on high until soft peaks form. Scrape the bowl and beat 2 minutes longer, until stiff peaks form. Fold the whipped topping into the cooled buttermilk mixture. Beat at high speed until smooth and creamy. Fold in the fruit. Spoon one-third of the filling into the bottom of a 3-quart bowl. Add half of the angel food cake pieces. Spread with half of the remaining filling. Layer with the remaining cake pieces and filling. Refrigerate several hours or overnight. Yields 12 servings.

Calories: 200; Fat: 2 g; Cholesterol: 3 mg; Sodium: 191 mg; Carbohydrates: 37 g; Fiber: 2 g; Diabetic Exchange: 1 fruit, 1 starch, ½ skim milk

DELICIOUS CHOCOLATE SAUCE

6   tablespoons cocoa
2   tablespoons plus 2 teaspoons cornstarch
⅔   cup instant nonfat dry milk
¼   teaspoon salt
3   cups water
2   tablespoons reduced-calorie margarine
1   tablespoon vanilla extract
20 individual packets sugar substitute

Assemble all ingredients and utensils. In a saucepan combine the cocoa, cornstarch, dry milk, and salt. Stir the water into the dry mixture until smooth. Add the margarine and cook over low heat, stirring constantly. Bring the mixture to a boil. Reduce the heat and simmer for 2 minutes, stirring constantly. Remove the pan from the heat. Add the vanilla and sugar substitute. Stir gently to mix. Store in a glass bowl in the refrigerator until ready to use. Reheat as needed. Yields 3 cups or 24 servings of 2 tablespoons each.

Calories: 21; Fat: 1 g; Cholesterol: 4 mg; Sodium: 37.8 mg;
Carbohydrates: 3 g; Fiber: 0 g; Diabetic Exchange: Free

LEMON SAUCE

2   *cups water*
2   *tablespoons cornstarch*
⅛   *teaspoon salt*
2   *tablespoons margarine*
2   *tablespoons lemon juice*
    Grated rind of 1 lemon
8   *individual packers of sugar substitute*

Assemble all ingredients and utensils. In a small saucepan combine the water, cornstarch, and salt. Stir until smooth. Cook and stir over medium heat until thickened and clear. Continue to simmer another 2 minutes. Remove the pan from the heat. Add the remaining ingredients and stir lightly to mix. Serve warm. Yields 2 cups or 8 servings of ¼ cup each.

Calories: 37; Fat: 3 g; Cholesterol: 0 mg; Sodium: 75 mg;
Carbohydrates: 3 g; Fiber: 0 g; Diabetic Exchange: 1 fat

STRAWBERRY SAUCE

½   *cup vanilla nonfat yogurt*
¼   *cup low-sugar strawberry jam*
1   *cup unsweetened frozen strawberries, thawed*

Assemble all ingredients and utensils. In a food processor beat the yogurt, jam, and strawberries until blended. Use the sauce for cakes, yogurt, or waffles. Yields 1½ cups or 6 servings of ¼ cup each.

Calories: 32; Fat: 0 g; Cholesterol: 4 mg; Sodium: 13 mg;
Carbohydrates: 7 g; Fiber: 0 g; Diabetic Exchange: ½ fruit

~⊱ *Appendix* ⊰~

THE DIABETIC EXCHANGE PROGRAM

*I*n the course of preparing a healthy lifestyle cookbook, I felt it was important to include information about the exchange lists prepared by the American Diabetes Association and the American Dietetic Association. The exchange program is often recommended by physicians and nutritionists for their diabetic patients, and it is a valid and simple method of diet planning for anyone who wishes to improve his or her diet. All of the recipes in this book include exchange information.

It is estimated that 14 million people in the United States have diabetes, but only half of these people know that they have it. Diabetes is a disorder characterized by the body's failure to properly convert glucose (the fuel derived from food) into energy. The body uses insulin, a hormone produced by the pancreas, to do this. But if the body does not produce insulin, or is unable to use the insulin properly, the result is high levels of glucose in the blood. The immediate consequences of this can be fatigue, excessive hunger and thirst, and frequent urination, as well as long-term complications.

Diabetes is diagnosed when levels of glucose in the blood are higher than normal. Acceptable levels are generally 80 to 120 mg/dl after fasting overnight. Different labs might have different levels depending on the equipment used.

All foods produce some glucose; however some foods will convert to more glucose than others during digestion. Following is a chart that indicates the percent of certain nutrients that are converted to glucose.

NUTRIENT	FOOD SOURCE	PERCENT CONVERTED
Carbohydrate	sugar and concentrated sweets, starches, fruit, and milk	100
Protein	meat, milk, and small amounts in bread and starch vegetables	60
Fats	oil, margarine, butter, fatty meat, salad dressings	10

As food is digested, glucose is released into the bloodstream for transport throughout the body, and the level of glucose in the bloodstream begins to rise. The pancreas produces insulin and releases it into the bloodstream with the glucose. Insulin lowers the level of glucose in the blood by allowing the glucose to leave the bloodstream and opening the cell to allow it to receive the glucose. The result: energy for the body.

Anything that interferes with this process—an absence of insulin, too little insulin, or cells that cannot use the insulin—will mean the level of glucose in the bloodstream will be too high. The result: diabetes.

TYPES OF DIABETES

Type I: Usually Type I diabetes will occur before age thirty. People with this type of diabetes have lost the ability to make any insulin as a result of damage to the cells of the pancreas. Only one tenth of all people with diabetes have Type I diabetes. Type I is treated with insulin, diet, and exercise.

Type II: Usually Type II diabetes occurs after age forty. People with this type of diabetes usually do make insulin; however, it may not be enough or the cells may not be able to use it properly. These people are probably not dependent on insulin to stay alive. However, they may need insulin to be healthier. Type II is treated with diet, exercise, and medication (if needed).

The ultimate goal of diabetes management is to maintain blood glucose levels in an acceptable range (doctors will determine that range for each individual). For many, especially with Type II diabetes, weight loss may be the first obstacle to tackle.

BASICS OF DIABETES MANAGEMENT

Exercise needs to be as much a part of diabetes care as diet or medication. Exercise not only helps with weight loss, but exercise alone helps reduce glucose levels. During exercise, the muscles are able to use more glucose with less insulin.

Exercise is recommended 3 to 5 times weekly for a duration of 30 to 45 minutes. Walking is considered an ideal exercise; however, your doctor should determine the proper amount of exercise and rate for you.

Medication is necessary for all people with Type I diabetes and most people with Type II diabetes. With very careful meal planning, weight control, and exercise, some with Type II diabetes may be able to manage without medicines.

Oral hypoglycemic agents are appropriate only for those who do make insulin (type II) These pills help the individual make insulin more effectively. If a maximum dose does not control glucose levels, insulin injections are necessary.

Insulin injections contain the same hormone produced by the body. Insulin must be injected into the body because it would be digested if swallowed and, therefore no longer work. The only difference in insulin made by the body and the type that is injected is that food must be matched to the amount given because it cannot be taken back or added to as it can in the body. All people with Type I diabetes and some with Type II diabetes will need insulin.

Diet: A meal plan is often given to people with diabetes for specific guidelines on how much food to eat, what type of food to eat, and when to eat. The "Diabetic Diet" is actually the same guidelines encouraged for all people and incorporates the guidelines previously discussed. The only added considerations are that amounts of foods are especially important, as well as the time of day each meal is eaten.

Preferably, a Registered Dietitian will evaluate your lifestyle, schedule, and nutrition needs. Your meal plan will be individually developed based on this information. Most meal plans incorporate the Diabetic Exchange Lists. These lists are similar to the groups listed in the Food Pyramid except that some portion sizes may be different or some foods may be classified differently based on the actual chemical make-up. A meal plan will assign the number of portions to eat from each food group at each meal.

As you can see, each food group has a wide variety of foods as well as serving sizes. A more complete list may be obtained from your registered dietitian or the American Diabetes Association, Inc., 1660 Duke Street, Alexandria, VA 22314. You can also telephone them at 1-800-DIABETES (342-2383) or visit them on the Web at www.diabetes.org.

Carbohydrate counting is gaining in popularity as an alternative to strictly using the Diabetic Exchange lists. This method is based on the exchange lists, but focuses on the carbohydrate content of foods with extra training in label reading for carbohydrate content.

Carbohydrate counting is used by almost all people who use insulin pumps, and by many other people taking insulin by shots daily. Most of these people find it gives more flexibility in meal planning, but it also takes additional training with a registered dietitian.

If you or a family member have diabetes and do not have a meal plan, or have not reviewed your meal plan with a dietitian in the past five years, speak to your doctor about this. Ask him to recommend someone, or phone your local hospital for information on how to make an appointment with a registered dietitian.

New research has found that the complications of diabetes may be minimized or avoided with good control of blood glucose levels. This can be achieved with dedication, good communication with your health care team, and following your prescribed therapy.

Diabetes does not go away, but it can be controlled relatively easily.

FOOD GROUPS	SAMPLES
Milk	1 cup skim milk
	1 cup buttermilk
Fruit	½ cup canned peaches
	1¼ cups fresh strawberries
	2 tablespoons raisins
Breads/starches	1 slice wheat bread
	½ cup bran cereal
	1 3-ounce baked potato
Vegetable	½ cup green beans
	1 cup raw broccoli
Meats:	
Lower fat	1 ounce chicken breast
	1 ounce lean beef
Higher fat	1 ounce prime rib
	1 tablespoon peanut butter

Fat	1 teaspoon regular margarine
	1 slice bacon
	1 tablespoon gravy

Exchange Lists

Exchange lists for meal planning prepared by the American Diabetes Association, the American Dietetic Association, and the U.S. Public Health Service have provided an effective guide for the selection of mealtime and snack foods for several decades. Foods are divided into six basic groups including milk, vegetable, fruit, bread (carbohydrates), meat, and fat exchanges. Each food in a group contains the same number of calories as other foods in that specific list. In the fruit exchange list, for example, one medium-sized apple has sixty calories, as do twelve grapes, one small nectarine, or one-half cup of orange juice, and so on. Using this system, you may choose from a variety of items when planning a meal or snack.

The amount of each food (or the number of exchanges) you may have depends on the total number of calories you need each day. Your personal physician or dietitian should help you set guidelines to meet your needs.

You will find the exchange lists easy, once you learn the trick.

Following is a list of the exchange groups and the chemical breakdown of one exchange for each.

GROUP	COMPOSITION
Milk	90 calories
	12 grams of carbohydrates
	8 grams of protein
	a trace of fat
Vegetable	25 calories
	5 grams of carbohydrates
	2 grams of protein
Fruit	60 calories
	15 grams of carbohydrates

Starch	80 calories
	15 grams of carbohydrates
	3 grams of protein
	a trace of fat
Meat (lower fat)	55 calories
	7 grams of protein
	3 grams of fat
Meat (medium fat)	75 calories
	7 grams of protein
	5 grams of fat
Meat (high fat)	100 calories
	7 grams of protein
	8 grams of fat
Fat	45 calories
	5 grams of fat

Free foods are fewer than 15 to 20 calories per serving. Limit free foods to a total of 50 to 60 calories per day divided among meals and snacks, rather than eating them all at one time.

References

About Fiber in Your Diet, Channing Bete Co., Inc., South Deerfield, MA: 1989.

American Institute for Cancer Research Newsletter. Issue 42, Winter, 1994.

The Diabetes Care Guide. New York: Health Care Publishing, 1993.

Eating for a Healthier Heart. Nashville: Baptist Hospital, 1992.

Fast Food Facts. Nashville: Morrison's Hospitality Group, 1993.

Fiber Facts. The American Dietetic Association, 1986.

Franz, Marion J. *Exchanges for All Occasions.* Wayzata, MN: International Diabetes Center, Inc., 1983.

Managing Your Diabetes. Indianapolis: Eli Lilly & Co., 1993.

Manual of Clinical Nutrition Management. Nashville: Morrison's Hospitality Group, 1993. Morrison's Nutro-Facts™ Computer Software Program.

Milchovich, Sue U. and Barbara Dunn-Long. *Diabetes Mellitus: A Practical Handbook.* Palo Alto: Bull Publishing Co., 1993.

Nutrition and your Health: Dietary Guidelines for Americans, 3rd Edition, U.S. Department of Agriculture, U.S. Department of Health and Human Services, 1990.

Position of the American Dietetic Association: Health Implications of Dietary Fiber. *Journal of the American Dietetic Association* 93 (1993): 1446-1447.

Salt, Sodium and Blood Pressure. American Heart Association, 1992.

Steps to a Healthy Heart. Nashville: Morrison's Hospitality Group, 1993.

Index

About the Author

Daisy King, known across the South as "Miss Daisy," is a well-established author whose cookbooks—including *Recipes from Miss Daisy's, The Original Tennessee Homecoming Cookbook, Miss Daisy Celebrates Tennessee, Miss Daisy's Blue Ribbon Desserts,* and *Gracious Entertaining, Southern Style*—have combined sales of more than 1.5 million copies. An author, restauranteur, food consultant, and home economist, she lives in Nashville, Tennessee.